Wolfgang von Erffa

UNCOMPROMISING TIBET

Culture - Religion - Politics

Paljor Publications

First published in German, 1992
EDITION INTERFROM, Zurich

English Revised Edition, 1996
Paljor Publications
D-39, Jangpura Extension
New Delhi - 14
India

ISBN: 81-86230-05-X

Photos: DIIR Archives, Dharamsala.

Published by Paljor Publications and printed at
Indraprastha Press (CBT), New Delhi, India.

CONTENTS

Publisher's Note

When 'Uncompromising Tibet' by Wolfgang von Erffa first appeared in German four years ago it was widely read and well received by both scholars interested in Tibet and by a growing general readership. Therefore we are pleased to publish the English translation of this valuable book in an updated and revised edition.

The author has very accurately conveyed the history of Tibet which, in itself proves the country's independent nationhood from the earliest records. Its relationship with neighbouring China, Nepal, India, Mongolia and Russia are outlined explicitly. The book tells us how Tibet has – since the beginning of history – relentlessly fought and negotiated with foreign powers in different eras and under varying circumstances to always emerge as a nation uncompromising on the question of its freedom. The symbiotic political and religious influence between Tibet and its neighbours during the course of Central Asia's rich and troubled history also makes an interesting study.

This book narrates the aftermath of China's occupation of Tibet, since 1959, and the continuing resistance of Tibetans to regain freedom and justice. Tibetan people have suffered and are still suffering under Chinese rule.

H.H. the Dalai Lama, the spiritual and temporal leader of the Tibetan people, is the living force behind the dream of freedom and peace for all Tibetans. Whatever the odds, Tibetans have adopted non-violence and compassion as a tool to negotiate with China. As obdurate and obstinate the Chinese stand may be, the world must see that truth and the force of compassion will prevail ultimately so that the tragedy of Tibet and the tragedy of Tiananmen massacre are not repeated.

It is our sincere hope that the book will serve as a guide and reference for everyone interested in Tibetan history and politics. We congratulate the author for his remarkable work.

1st June 1996

Tsewang Gyalpo

Dedicated
to the future enlightened and compassionate leaders
of China, who will end the sufferings of the Tibetan
people, meet their just aspirations, and hence ensure
the reemergence of Tibet as a friend of China.

Victorious in all directions: National Symbol

Escape into India, 1959

From Left: Panchen Lama, Dalai Lama, Chou-en lai, Nehru and Indra Gandhi, 1956, India

UNDER THE SPELL OF UNCOMPROMISING TIBET

When the Dalai Lama was forced to escape in 1959 from Lhasa to India, after the rebellion of the Tibetans against the Chinese, I was only a schoolboy. Instead of being attentive in class I began to dream of Tibet. I studied accurate maps in an atlas of 1899 in which, two generations earlier, somebody had pencilled an itinerary through the Himalayas to Tibet. I read everything about Tibet that I was able to find and studied in depth the works of some of the important researchers on Tibet; the brothers Schlagintweit and Sven Hedin, as well as the accounts of Heinrich Harrer. As yet I felt only an uncertain longing to follow their example, although I had slender hopes of doing so: I had fallen under Tibet's spell.

Years later an event — itself insignificant — remained in my memory: In 1973, I visited the opera in Prague for a performance of Verdi's *Nabucco*. The thunderous applause which followed the chorus of liberty did not end; the enthusiastic audience applauded for eleven minutes. Five years after Russian tanks had cracked down on "Prague's spring" this was perhaps the only opportunity for the expression of a political opinion. The agents of the KGB either did not attend opera performances or did not understand Italian.

Melody and applause had a long resonance. The nostalgia for freedom would engage me for a long time.

In 1983, exactly ten years later, I met the XIV Dalai Lama for the first time. It happened in Singapore. I observed his great radiation on people, on an audience of thousands, who listened to his public addresses. The deep sympathy which he encountered, and encounters today, may be a resonance of the dignified majesty of his appearance as the God-king of Tibet. Mainly, however, it is a reflection of his great cordiality as a simple monk with a special vocation for compassion. After that first personal meeting I became aware that the Dalai Lama is also one of the great mystics of our time. It was only later that I met another great mystic, whose work everywhere has found special recognition, Mother Teresa. Like the Dalai Lama she possesses a great force of radiation, which captures people and causes their hearts to burn with compassion.

At the time of my first encounter with the Dalai Lama I was working for a German political foundation in Asia. I took a special interest in the influence of religion on politics. The triumphant victory of the Catholic faith over Marxism-Leninism in Poland and its role in the conservation of the national identity in the face of domination by the Soviet Union appeared to me exemplary.

I studied the question of whether the strength of Buddhist belief can constitute the foundation of a religious fundamentalism with political dynamics. I was concerned to develop concepts which could be applied in projects for the renaissance of Buddhism and the preservation of the national identity in the camps of the Khmer refugees and displaced persons on the Thai-Cambodian border.

At the same time I began to become more closely involved with Tibet. Several meetings with the Dalai Lama in Dharamsala in India followed.

I then decided to work for a while as a free-lance writer and journalist. Finally I had the time to concentrate fully on questions which wholly captured my attention.

I wrote books on politics and religion in Asia, on Cambodia, and about China and Afghanistan. Increasingly, however, I concentrated on Tibet. I was fascinated by the uniqueness of the magnificent centuries-old civilisation on the roof of the world, which has resisted for more than a quarter of a century all attempts by the Chinese invaders to destroy it. I visited Tibet and the countries and regions where the Buddhists venerate the Dalai Lama as their religious head, namely Ladakh, Nepal, Outer Mongolia and Buryatia in Siberia. I travelled through China, Viet Nam and South Korea, where Mahayana Buddhism remains a significant force.

When the democracy movement of China succumbed to gunfire on the Square of Heavenly Peace in Peking, but only a few months later the Marxist-Leninist dictatorships in Eastern Europe collapsed one after the other, I tried to analyse this triumph of non-violent struggle for liberty.

The Chinese occupying troops and the Chinese colonial policy do not have the power to overcome the spirit of liberty in Tibet, they have not succeeded in destroying religion and culture completely.

This book attempts to describe the background to these dramatic events and to trace a perspective for the future. It is a testimony of the uncompromising Tibet, of the invincible desire of the Tibetans for liberty, of the radiation and force of their religion and culture which is in the process of triumphing over Communism, and which could in future again become influential, also in China.

On a beautiful summer day in 1993 the Dalai Lama was joined by numerous friends of Tibet, including Heinrich Harrer, on a boat trip on a lake in the South of Bavaria. At that occasion I presented a copy of the

German edition of this book to the Dalai Lama. He asked for the meaning of the title in English. "Uncompromising Tibet, that is very good", he remarked.

I wish to thank all Tibetans and friends of Tibet who replied with great patience to all my questions and gave me advice. I would like especially to thank Tsewang Norbu, the Chairman of the German-Tibetan Cultural Society, who has checked this manuscript critically. I also very cordially thank Marie-Luise Broch, Geneva, and Jane Perkins, Dharamsala, for the comprehensive information which they provided to me over many years.

TRIUMPH OF COMPASSION

"When the metal bird flies and horses roll on wheels, Tibetans will be spread over the world like ants, and the teaching of Buddha will come to the most distant countries."

Padmasambhava, Indian Tantric master and supreme spiritual guardian of Tibet, 8th century

Victorious in all Directions

During a visit at his residence in exile in Dharamsala the XIV Dalai Lama gave me a small gift, a Tibetan coin, minted at the beginning of the twentieth century, "as a souvenir", he said, with a cordial smile.

One side of the coin is adorned by the perfect form of the lotus flower, on the other side ingenious Tibetan letters declare: "Victorious in all Directions".

The meaning of this inscription surprised me: Tibet, the Government in Exile of the Dalai Lama, remained not victorious at all against the overwhelming might of the Chinese, who had occupied part of the country in 1949 and the whole of it in 1959 and incorporated Tibet into the territory of the People's Republic of China by cruel oppression. The Chinese tried to humiliate this beautiful country on the roof of the world, to destroy its unique culture and to substitute for its religion the ideology of Marxism-Leninism, mixed with the thoughts of Mao Zedong. This attempt caused the death of 1.2 million people, approximately one fifth of the entire population of Tibet. The Tibetans were not able to preserve their liberty against the immense military might of "The Middle Kingdom".

With the granting of the Nobel Peace Prize to the Dalai Lama in December 1989, the attention of the world was suddenly focused on the God-king of Tibet and on the fate of his country. At once the incredible spiritual force of the religion of the Tibetans, Mahayana Buddhism, became evident: did religion not triumph in spite of all oppression and did it not definitely defeat the pretensions of Marxist-Leninist ideology? The failure of the *raison d'être* of the ideological pretensions of the People's Republic of China could not fail to have consequences for the self-consciousness of the aged leaders in Peking. The Communist ideology — on the basis of which China emerged forty years ago to transform a "World of Darkness" into a "World of Light" — lost its vigour and strength. These proud words of Mao Zedong on the creation of the People's Republic — "China rises" — appear today completely meaningless, very distant and very unreal. This is due to the revolution of 1989.

Buddhism — which Mao Zedong characterised as poison in a comment to the Dalai Lama, which had already poisoned Tibet and Outer Mongolia — reached its apogee in Tibet. In other regions of Central Asia which were traditionally Buddhist, as in Outer Mongolia, Buddhism remained very strong, and in other very distant countries, in Europe and in America, interest in the Tibetan school of Buddhism increased. Guru Padmasambhava, the Indian pandit, who introduced the tantric form of Tibetan Buddhism into Tibet in the eighth century made the following prophecy: "When the metal bird flies and horses roll on wheels, Tibetans will be spread over the world like ants, and the teaching of Buddha will come to the most distant countries."

Today, there are more than 500 Buddhist centres outside Tibet, many in Europe and North America.

While the material structures of Tibetan Buddhist religion and culture to a large extent were destroyed, the ideas and convictions of this religion were strengthened by this destruction.

Against this background the inscription on the coin of the Dalai Lama "Victorious in all Directions" seems to gain a special significance for our time.

Omnipresence of Chenrezig, Bodhisattva of Compassion

Statues of Chenrezig, Bodhisattva of Compassion, abound in the temples of Mahayana Buddhism and in shops owned by Chinese traders, not only in China, Taiwan, Hong Kong and Singapore, but also in Japan, Korea, Vietnam as well as among the ethnic Chinese in Thailand and Malaysia. The Chinese name of this Bodhisattva is Kuan-yin, in Sanskrit Avalokiteshvara. The Dalai Lama together with his thirteen predecessors are considered to be reincarnations of this divinity of compassion. The boundless compassion is symbolised in some of the sculptures by a thousand eyes and arms, which Chenrezig requires to hand out benefactions to the needy.

Mahayana Buddhism was once the most important religion in China. We have little reason to doubt the possibility that in a not too distant future the divinity of compassion may triumph again in China, and that the symbol of the lotus flower, represented on the coin of the Dalai Lama, could regain its special significance for hundreds of millions of the 1.1 billion inhabitants of the People's Republic of China.

The emperors of the Manchurian Qing Dynasty, who ruled The Middle Kingdom until 1911, were considered reincarnations of Manjushri, Bodhisattva of Wisdom. Manjushri is represented holding a flaming sword in his right hand, which cuts through ignorance, and holding a lotus flower with a representation of the Wisdom-Scripture in his left hand.

The rulers of the previous Mongolian Dynasty, the heirs of Ghengis Khan, were considered reincarnations of Vajrapani, Bodhisattva of Energy and Power. Vajrapani is represented standing on the disc of the sun, holding a *vajra*, a ritual thunderbolt, in his right hand.

Avalokitesvara, Vajrapani and Manjushri are often represented in trinity: divinities, whose reincarnations were supposed – and in the case of Tibet still are supposed – to be the secular rulers of Tibet, Mongolia and China. Avalokitesvara, divinity of boundless compassion, is considered to be the most important of those reincarnations. This explains the special role of the Dalai Lamas in Tibet, Mongolia and China in the past and today.

Dalai Lamas as Spiritual Advisors to the Chinese Emperors

The historical dimension of the relationship between Dalai Lamas and Chinese emperors proves to be fascinating. This special relationship is not unlike the relations between the Popes and the Emperors of the Holy Roman Empire of the German Nation. The origin of this special relationship can be traced back centuries: The grandson of Ghengis Khan, Kublai Khan, the first emperor of the Mongolian Yuan Dynasty, was very much impressed by the personality of a high Tibetan lama, Phagpa. He made him his spiritual and religious advisor. Phagpa had arrived as a ten-year-old novice together with Sakya Pandita, abbot of the Sakya monastery in Southern Central Tibet, at the court of Prince Gödan in the region of Kokonor. Sakya Pandita instructed the Mongolian ruler in the teachings of Buddha. Later on the nineteen-year-old monk Phagpa became the religious teacher of Kublai Khan, successor to Prince Gödan.

In 1254 Phagpa received a letter from Kublai Khan, in which he was endowed with the highest authority over Tibet. The letter reads:

"As a true believer in the Great Lord Buddha, the all-merciful and invincible ruler of the world, whose presence, like the sun, lights up every dark place, I have always shown special favour to the monks and monasteries of your country. Having faith in Lord Buddha, I studied the teachings of your uncle, Sakya Pandita, and in the year of the Water-Ox, I received your own teachings. After studying under you, I have been encouraged to continue helping your monks and monasteries, and in return for what I have learnt from your teachings, I must make you a gift. This letter, then, is my present. It grants you authority over all Tibet, enabling you to protect the religious institutions and faith of your people and to propagate Lord Buddha's teachings."

In 1260, after the death of Monka Khan, Kublai Khan became ruler of Mongolia. Phagpa presided over the ceremonies of the enthronement. At this time it was said that the relationship between Lama and Patron, between the Tibetan Lama and the Mongolian Khan, was like the "sun and moon in heaven".

The Tibetan word for this close relationship was "Chö-Yön", which means: Lama-Patron or Priest-Patron relationship. It incorporates elements of the institution of the protectorate according to international public law which developed on the basis of Western conceptions.

In this special relationship, which embodies a duality of secular and of spiritual rule, a dependency between Ruler and Lama is established. Furthermore, the idea of the universal Buddhist Emperorship of the

Chakravartirajas of India incorporates a kind of spiritual justification for the imperial rule. This sacred dimension of the justification of his rule may have served Kublai Khan in his efforts to be generally accepted as Emperor of China. The sacred claim to be Buddhist Universal Emperor was considered as legitimation for the rule not only over Mongolia, Tibet and China, but over the entire world. In this respect the name "Yuan", which Kublai Khan gave to his dynasty, is interesting. This word derives from "Qianyuan", which means "original creative force".

In 1260 Kublai Khan granted Phagpa the title "Preceptor of the Empire". Furthermore he received secular authority over the Tibetan provinces Ü-Tsang, Dotod (Kham) and Domed (Amdo). There are reports that Kublai Khan — influenced by Phagpa — forbade the throwing of Chinese into rivers and drowning them. This practice was meant to reduce a too rapid increase in the Chinese population in Mongolia, which was thought to endanger the power of the dynasty of Kublai Khan.

Phagpa was also successful in convincing Kublai Khan to grant permission to practice their religion not only to his own Sakya school of Buddhism, but also to the other Buddhist schools. Hence Phagpa gained sympathy and support from the other abbots and religious rulers in Tibet. A Tibetan lama of the Kagyü school taught at the same time at the court of Kublai Khan.

Phagpa mentions in his memoirs that in 1271 he met there a stranger who had travelled from very far. This may have been Marco Polo, who frequented the court of Kublai Khan, and who himself reported that he had met the Lama of the Khan.

In 1280, when Phagpa died in the Sakya monastery,

i.e. when he probably was poisoned, Kublai Khan had conquered almost the whole of China. He mounted the throne as emperor of China.

While Kublai Khan had favoured the Sakya school, in 1331 one of his successors called a lama who headed the Karma Kagyü school, Karmapa Rangjung Dorje, to his court. In 1333 he presided over the ceremonies of the imperial coronation of Togon Temür.

The Chö-Yön relationship, which originated as a religio-political relationship between the Tibetan Lama and the Mongolian Ruler, lasted several centuries. Later on it continued between the Manchu Emperors and the Dalai Lamas. Only in 1911, with the fall of the Qing Dynasty, did the Dalai Lama terminate the relationship.

During the Ming Dynasty(1368-1644) the Chö-Yön relationship was discontinued. At the same time, however, the special relationship with the Mongols, especially towards the Mongol ruler, Altan Khan, was maintained.

The grandson of Altan Khan, Yönten Gyatso, born in 1589 in Mongolia, was recognised as a reincarnation of the III Dalai Lama. He received a special religious education from Tibetan teachers in Mongolia and became the IV Dalai Lama. The spiritual relationship between Mongolia and Tibet deepened, and the Gelugpa school, to which the Dalai Lamas belonged, gained special importance.

In 1644 the Manchu Dynasty took over in China. Emperor Shun-chih invited the V Dalai Lama to visit his court. There was a prediction from the previous century, dating from 1578, that the descendants of the Mongolian ruler Altan Khan would after eighty years rise to be the supreme rulers of Mongolia and China. As the Tibetans considered the Mongols and Manchus to be close relatives, they believed that the prophecy was fulfilled when the first emperor of the Manchu dynasty ascended to the throne.

From 1652 to 1653 the V Dalai Lama travelled to China. The Chinese emperor set out to meet him. There was a first encounter on Chinese territory, in close vicinity of the Tibetan border. Later on, in Peking, splendid ceremonies were held. The emperor had ordered the construction of a special palace for the Dalai Lama, the Huan Ssu (Yellow Palace). In the audience hall the Emperor and the Dalai Lama exchanged presents during the official ceremony — inter-alia — golden plates, on which the titles were engraved, which they had respectively bestowed on each other. The title for the Dalai Lama was: Great Master, Supreme One, God of the Firmament, Bodhisattva.

During the Manchurian Qing Dynasty, from 1644 to 1911, the Chö-Yön relationship existed officially and with legal validity. During this time the Dalai Lamas were almost without interruption spiritual and religious advisors to the Chinese emperors, and they in return, were protectors and patrons of Buddhism in the Middle Empire and in Tibet. The God-kings of Tibet were in the position to ask the emperors of China for military assistance. A good example in this respect are the events in 1718, when the troops of the Manchu emperor helped to expel the Dzungars, who had occupied Lhasa. The VII Dalaï Lama was able to return to Lhasa and again exercise his legitimate rule over Tibet.

The situation before the end of the Manchu Dynasty was quite different. In 1909 in Peking the XIII Dalai Lama still presided over the Buddhist funeral ritual for the Emperor Kuang Hsu and the Empress-Dowager, who had died one day after the emperor. One year later relations between Tibet and China considerably deteriorated. Already in previous years Chinese troops had been able to conquer parts of Eastern Tibet. In 1910 they invaded Lhasa and shelled the Jokhang temple as well as the Potala palace. The XIII Dalai Lama was able to escape across the border and to find refuge in Darjeeling, India. The Chinese government in Peking declared the Dalai Lama deposed.

Because of the unanimous resistance of the Tibetan population the Chinese were, however, compelled to give in. The Amban (representative of the Chinese government in Lhasa) Lien-yü invited the Panchen Lama to come from Shigatse to Lhasa. He lived in the Norbulingka Palace, the Summer Palace of the Dalai Lama. The inhabitants of Lhasa protested. When Sun Yat-sen overthrew the Manchu Dynasty in China in 1911, the soldiers of the Chinese garrison in Lhasa revolted against the representative of the Manchu Dynasty, the Amban. He escaped and found refuge in Shigatse. Followers of the Dalai Lama succeeded in expelling the Chinese from Lhasa and Shigatse. There was very hard fighting for Lhasa. In 1912 the Chinese President, Yüan Shih-kai, ordered the Amban in Lhasa to send the Chinese troops back to China. This was, however, impossible because all roads from Tibet to China were blocked by Tibetan troops. The Chinese troops finally capitulated and were able to leave unimpeded.

The President of China sent the Dalai Lama a telegram, in which he excused himself for the excesses of the Chinese troops and assured the Dalai Lama of reinstatement in his previous position. The Dalai Lama replied that he did not ask the Chinese government for any position because he himself was now going to exercise both secular and spiritual power in Tibet.

This declaration is considered to be a formal termination of the Chö-Yön relationship: China had violated her obligations under this relationship to act as protector of Tibet. It had become evident already before, during the Chinese invasion of Tibet, that neither the Emperor nor the Empress-Dowager were still willing to assume the role of protector of Tibet. Hence the Dalai Lama was no longer in the position to remain as spiritual and religious advisor to the Emperor.

Some historians and specialists in international public law argue that China, as a kind of compensation for her duty to provide military protection, was entitled to exercise certain rights over Tibet, i.e. suzerainty, but not sovereignty. The Dalai Lamas always maintained the power to rule in Tibet.

It would not be unreasonable to state that, as opposed to the Chinese claim that Tibet is and has always been a part of China, China has been and remains — at least to a certain extent from a spiritual and religious viewpoint a part of Tibet.

The German edition of the memoirs of the last emperor of the Manchurian dynasty, the "child-emperor" Pu Yi, reproduces a photograph showing his mother Tzu Hsi, the Empress-Dowager, posing dressed as the divinity of mercy, i.e. as Avalokiteshvara, the reincarnation of whom the Dalai Lama is believed to be. Hence the influence of Tibet in China was considerable. An advisor in the Government-in-Exile of the Dalai Lama explained to me his view that, at the beginning of our century in the Chinese empire, the Manchu Dynasty favoured Tibetan officials as compared to Han Chinese. In this fact he saw a subconscious reason for the resentment of the Han Chinese towards the

15

Tibetans, from which flowed their colonial policy towards Tibet based on hatred.

In 1951 again Chinese soldiers arrived in Lhasa. The Tibetans did not show them friendly feelings. The Dalai Lama mentions in his autobiography (1990) that Tibetans demonstrated again and again their contempt towards the Chinese. Wherever they saw Chinese soldiers the Tibetans clapped their hands and spat. Children threw stones and monks knotted loose parts of their robes into a bunch to hit Chinese soldiers who approached them.

The Dalai Lama recalls, however, that — while a few thousand out of hundreds of millions of Chinese were guilty of cruelties towards the Tibetans — at the same time a few million Chinese certainly acted in a friendly manner.

Manjushri — Wisdom reincarnated: Buddhism in China

Wutai Shan, the holy mountain in the province Shanxi, was the centre of the cult of Manjushri, Boddhisattva of Wisdom, of whom the emperor of the Manchu Dynasty was supposed to be a reincarnation. The highest of the five summits of Wutai Shan reaches 3,000 meters. It is considered to be the "roof" of Northern China. For Tibetan Buddhists Wutai Shan is the holiest place in China.

The XIII Dalai Lama visited Wutai Shan in 1908 and spent five months there. He payed homage to Manjushri. During this time a number of Mongolian tribal chiefs arrived to ask for his benediction.

There was also a mysterious visitor from Germany,

thought to be a German doctor. He may, however, not have been a medical doctor, but a visitor using his academic title of Ph.D. He presented the Dalai Lama with an illustrated book showing the arsenal of German weapons to demonstrate that Germany was prepared to help Tibet with arms. The Dalai Lama ignored this offer.

The temple of Wutai Shan was built 600 years ago, when Buddhism had great influence in China. The Tibetans believe that at least 100 million Chinese are Buddhists today.

Buddhism came to China at an early stage. According to a legend, Emperor Ming Ti in the first century A.D. had a significant dream. He saw a great, golden body in the air above the imperial palace. The head radiated interior fire and the body reflected the splendour of the moon and the sun. One of the imperial ministers interpreted the dream. The splendour resulted from the foundation of a new religion by Gautama Buddha in the West. Emperor Ming Ti sent a mission to India in order to ask Buddhist teachers to come to China.

By the middle of the third century A.D. there were already Buddhists everywhere in China. In the fifth century Buddhism spread strongly in China.

Albert Schweitzer describes in his book *The Weltanschauung of the Philosophers of India*, that the Chinese were especially moved by the generosity and inwardness of the ethics of compassion. Buddhism met the religious needs of the Chinese, which Confucianism had totally ignored and to which Taoism offered little.

In the ninth century A.D. Buddhism was – as well as other alien religions, i.e. Manicheism and the religion of Zarathustra – severely persecuted. In the eleventh century, when the pious Emperor Tsen-Tsung of the

17

Sung Dynasty granted Buddhism full religious liberty, 230,000 men and 15,000 women suddenly entered monasteries.

While Buddhism grew strong during the Mongolian Yuan Dynasty, its influence declined during the Ming Dynasty and during the Manchurian Qing Dynasty, inspite of the fact that the Manchu Emperors were considered to be reincarnations of Manjushri.

Lama Anagarika Govinda, son of a German father and a Bolivian mother, writes in his book *The Way of the White Clouds,* that nobody yet came to Tibet without falling under her spell, and that perhaps the ideas of the Chinese could be changed by the teachings of Buddha as once the ideas of the Mongolians had been.

Vajrapani – Reincarnation of Power: Freedom for Outer Mongolia

The secular rulers of Genghis Khan's Dynasty in Mongolia were for centuries considered to be reincarnations of Vajrapani, Bodhisattva of Energy and Power. This was certainly an asset for the consolidation of power over the Mongols who, since the thirteenth century, had converted from Shamanism and partly also from Nestorian Christianity to Buddhism.

Since the seventeenth century the head of the lamaist clergy in Mongolia, Bogdo Gegen Jetsundamba Khutukhtu, has been considered as reincarnation of Taranatha (1575-1634). This famous Tibetan monk and historian lived in the Jomonang monastery near Shigatse, whose abbot had in the fourteenth century created a philosophy of the void.

In September 1991 the Dalai Lama confirmed the

Tibetan monk Jampel Namdrol Chökyi Gyaltsen as the IX Jetsundampa Khutukhtu, i.e. the reincarnation of Taranatha. Jampel Namdrol, who was born on the eighth day of the eleventh month of the Water Monkey year, i.e. 1932, in Lhasa, fled to India following the invasion of the Chinese. He now lives at the Mainpat settlement of the Tibetan refugees in India. There are preparations for his return to Mongolia. Reting Rinpoche, the Regent of Tibet before the enthronement of the XIV Dalai Lama, had already recognised him as the IX Jetsundamba Khutukhtu.

The influence of Buddhism in Mongolia coincided with the conversion of Kublai Khan. From the sixteenth century onwards Buddhism was the state religion. The emperor of the Manchu Dynasty issued a decree in 1757, allowing the search for reincarnations of Jetsundamba Khutukthu only in Tibet.

In 1911 the VIII Jetsundamba Khutukhtu declared the independence of Mongolia from China. In 1919 China used force against Outer Mongolia by sending troops. The Chinese general Su Schu tsch'eng occupied Urga. Peking urged the settlement of debts arising from demands for reparations relating to the time after the Chinese revolution of 1911. China tried to enforce the same status on Outer Mongolia as she had forced upon Inner Mongolia.

There was an interlude, when in 1921 the Baltic Baron Niclas von Ungern-Sternberg, Lieutenant-General of the Asian Cavalry Division and Commander of the Detachment of Cossacks of the Imperial Russian Army, conquered the town of Urga, which is now named Ulan Bator. His 5,000 troops were composed of Russians, Buriats, Mongols and Tibetans.

Ungern-Sternberg was a Buddhist. He believed in

prophecies and lived under the delusion that he was the reincarnation of a martial god himself. He put faith in a legend according to which his family descended from the Huns, even from Attila himself. Hence he believed he had been chosen for his role in Mongolia. He married a Mongolian princess.

Ungern-Sternberg terminated the Chinese influence in Mongolia and reinstalled the VIII Jetsundamba Khutukhtu as official Head of State. The Baltic baron had the support of Japan, but he remained in power for only five months. Soviet and Mongolian troops conquered Urga in July of 1921. Outer Mongolia passed for seventy years under the hold of the Soviet-Union. The Jetsundamba Khutukhtu was allowed to keep his position as Head of State, bearing the title "Khan". After his death in 1924 it was forbidden to search for reincarnations.

The Dalai Lama visited Ulan Bator in 1982. There was an outbreak of enthusiastic manifestations of religious belief and attachment towards the Dalai Lama, in spite of sixty five years of Marxist-Leninist propaganda and anti-religious policy.

Today, monks again say their prayers in Erdene dsuu, once one of the most important Buddhist centres in the world. The monastery is situated in the immediate vicinity of Karakoram, the former capital of the Mongolian empire. Nothing more than a turtle in stone remains of the former grandeur: a symbol, indeed of its longevity.

From a wooden building near the main temple of Erdene dsuu two young monks intone strange, but melodious sounds with their horns — made of conch shells. It is the call to prayers. About forty monks assemble in the main building, the Mahakala temple.

They sit in four rows, two rows facing each other. The abbot, about eighty years of age, intones a mantra, other lamas, many older than eighty years, as well as a number of novices, the youngest only seven years old, join him in murmuring the prayer. A photograph of the Dalai Lama is put on the altar next to the statue of Buddha. Precious *thangkas* are placed on the side-walls, each with a frightening picture in gold of the powerful protectress Mahakala against a black background. An old monk with a very impressive face sits in the first row to the left. He holds in his hand a Vajra, a thunderbolt, which he moves each four minutes according to a tantric ritual to the sounds of gongs and drums. For a while I remain absorbed in the contemplation of this ritual; the very ancient ceremonies are touching and magnificent.

After the collapse of the Marxist-Leninist regimes in Eastern Europe and the Soviet Union the thaw also reached Mongolia. The country experienced a revival of Buddhism. The monks had been persecuted and murdered since the late thirties in Stalinist waves of terror. A large number of the monasteries, probably about 700, were systematically destroyed. Sixty years ago Erdene dsuu alone had more than 100 monasteries.

Ninety percent of the population of 2.2 million people in Mongolia are believed to be Buddhists. In early 1991 only one monastery was open in the entire country, the Ganden monastery in Ulan Bator. Believers had no possibility to practice their religion. In the meantime far more than 100 monasteries are supposed to have been re-established. Statues of Buddha as well as *thangkas*, previously hidden, have reappeared and are prominently displayed in the monasteries.

The Dalai Lama revisited Mongolia in 1991. About

15,000 people had assembled in front of Ganden monastery to welcome their spiritual leader with boundless enthusiasm. The Dalai Lama taught about the Lam-Rim principles (steps on the path to enlightenment) in a stadium to about 40,000 people.

He then addressed journalists in a speech, in which he emphasised that the human spirit is much stronger than all weapons.

The energy and power of Vajrapani live on.

White Tara and the Tzar: Lamas in Siberia and Saint Petersburg

The Buryats — who are ethnic Mongolians — had good relations with the last Russian Tzar, Nicholas II. He consented to the wish of the XIII Dalai Lama and authorised the construction of a lamaist temple in Saint Petersburg. The style of this temple, dedicated to the deity Kalachakra, is clearly influenced by Art Deco. A prominent artist, Nicholas Roerich, took part in its decoration. In the interior hall, glass windows painted by him with Buddhist symbols, can still be seen. In 1913, the ter-centenary of the Romanov Dynasty, was celebrated here in the presence of the envoys of the Buddhist states Siam and Mongolia.

The Buryat lamas considered the Tzar as a reincarnation of the White Tara, who represents the fertile aspects of compassion. According to a legend the White Tara originated from a tear of compassion from Avalokiteshvara's eye. She is depicted seated on a lotus flower in front of disks of the sun and moon, possessing seven eyes, three in the face, two in the hands, and two on the soles of her feet.

It may seem a little far-fetched to consider the Russian Orthodox ruler of Russia as her reincarnation. But this assumption certainly contributed to strengthening the links between the Tzar and his Buddhist subjects in the Eastern part of the empire.

Agwan Dorzhiev, a dynamic lama from the Buryat region of Siberia, educated in Drepung monastery close to Lhasa, who had been a teacher to the XIII Dalai Lama, was the moving force in the construction of the temple. In subsequent years he had several meetings with Tzar Nicolas II.

The orthodox church in Saint Petersburg, however, considered the influence of the Buddhist lamas on the Tzar with uneasiness, especially that of Agwan Dorzhiev. This Buryat lama had been able to gain a position similar to that of Rasputin. The Tzar, and especially the Tzarina, were receptive to the mystical aspects of Buddhism. They had confidence in the Tibetan medicine which Dorzhiev practiced. Because the imperial couple did not have a son, Dorzhiev was asked to carry out certain rituals, in order to cause such a joyful event. An heir to the throne, Tsarevich Alexei, was indeed born; however, he suffered from haemophilia.

Agwan Dorzhiev played an important role in the "Great Game" between Russia and England for the control of Asia. He was the official envoy of Tibet to the Imperial Court.

The British took the relations between the official envoy of the Dalai Lama and the Tzar, as well as the alleged supply of Russian weapons to the Tibetans, as a pretext for their military intervention in Tibet, the so-called Younghusband Expedition. Dorzhiev is believed to have travelled in 1911 to France, Germany and Italy with the task of asking for support for the independence of Mongolia and Tibet. Apparently he did not arouse much interest. Dorzhiev did indeed make an effort to move the Tzar to grant Russian protection against the English efforts. This must have appeared logical, following the British military expedition of 1904 to Lhasa.

For the Buddhists and for the temple times became more severe after the 1917 October Revolution in Russia. The monks followed advice from circles in the new government and painted a second layer of black pigment over the golden colour on the external walls of the temple. Today, seventy years later, the gold is reappearing at many spots. The former splendour could soon radiate again.

Presumably Dorzhiev was for some time an advisor to Lenin. He wrote a book on Buddhism and socialism, in which he tried to combine both teachings. At the end of the 1930s he was imprisoned in the course of Stalin's repression of the religious communities. He died in prison at the age of eighty seven.

Today's abbot, Lama Samayev Tenzin-Khetsun, confidently explained to me the future task of his temple: Buddhism appeared appropriate to help in filling the spiritual and ideological vacuum after the breakdown of Marxism-Leninism. He saw a sizeable interest in Buddhism among Russian intellectuals.

In Russia not only the Buryats, but also the Kalmyks are followers of the Dalai Lama. During the Second World War they sided with the Germans. Germany had promised them an independent state. Kalmyk regiments fought against Stalin's Red Army. As a punishment they were expelled from their areas of settlement on the Southern Volga to Siberia. Many Kalmyks perished during this forced resettlement.

The hospitality of the Mongolian Buryats in Ulan Ude, in Southern Siberia, on the border of Mongolia, is phenomenal. Already in the morning guests are honoured by numerous cheerful toasts. After the fourth glass of vodka my host, a retired colonel from the Red Army, became quite talkative. His German was rather fluent. He had served in Ulan Bator and in Potsdam. He knew Thuringia well and mentioned the small towns of Pössneck and Rudolstadt. While on the television — which in Buryat houses too is switched on from morning till evening — a pianist played Beethoven's *Appassionata*, the colonel, who was aware of my interest in Buddhism, drew my attention to a photograph of the Dalai Lama, which was fixed above a Persian wall carpet, made in the former GDR. Like a talisman this picture had accompanied the officer to all his duty stations, to Ulan Bator, Potsdam and Thuringia.

Photographs of the Dalai Lama seem to be omnipresent among the Buryats, like a testimony to a distant past. There is, however, hardly any knowledge left about Buddhism. In more than seventy years of Marxist-Leninist indoctrination, the secularization of society has been successful to a large extent.

In the house of a prominent Buryat opera singer, Kim Bazarsadaev, who in addition to great opera roles liked to sing an ode to Lenin, a picture of the Dalai Lama is also displayed prominently in the living room.

I was not the only guest. A high Kalmyk lama also arrived. He had come for the cremation of the Bandido Khambo Lama, the highest Buddhist dignitary of Siberia, Choj Dorje Budaev, who had recently died. His monastery, Datsan, is some forty kilometers north of Ulan Ude, east of Lake Baikal In the beginning of the 1940s Stalin allowed the re-establishment of this monastery. After the radical persecution of all religions in the Soviet Union in the 1930s, to which practically all Buddhist monks succumbed, i.e. were murdered or perished in *GULAGS*, the dictator suddenly discovered the "value" of religion: The objective was to use it to strengthen the spirit of resistance of the people in the Second World War.

When I visited the monastery, a monk explained the obstacles which the Buddhist faith encounters today: during Communist rule all restrictions were directed towards the interdiction of individual thinking. In addition, with the assassination of the lamas, knowledge of Buddhism was to a large extent eliminated. Now the main task of the monks consisted in explaining to the people the essence of the Buddhist faith. The monk mentioned that there were again fourteen Buddhist centres in the region of Buryatia. Before the October Revolution in 1917, forty four temples had existed; all were destroyed.

Only 250,000 Buryats live in their old settlement area around Ulan Ude. They became a minority in their own country as compared to the 750,000 Russians.

In the summer of 1992 the monastery lived in expectation of the impending visit of the Dalai Lama who was supposed to come in October. Already in 1982 and 1991 the Supreme Head of the Tibetan, Mongolian, Buryat and Kalmyk Buddhists had visited Siberia.

TIBET'S SPIRITUALITY

"Blessed be your speech, body and soul by the jewel of the lotus flower."
Tibetan Mantra

Om Mani Padme Hum

The inscription *Om mani padme hum* is engraved on innumerable mani stones in Tibet and along the paths of pilgrims in the Himalayan countries marked by Buddhism. Pious Tibetans daily move hundreds of thousands of prayer mills, murmuring this mantra. "Oh jewel in the mystery of the lotus flower" is the popular translation.

Another translation better reflects the true meaning: "Blessed be your speech, body and soul by the jewel of the lotus flower."

In fighting for their survival, it is the fate of many Tibetans, especially the nomads, to wander continuously. They are forced to do so because of the scarcity of pastures. During such long journeys, or during rides through the magnificent, but also monotonous expanses, it is only natural that the thoughts of men should be different as compared to those of people in the narrowness of cities or in a densely populated countryside. Thoughts seem to vanish in the unlimited vastness to enter upon ways and wrong ways, far from the right path leading to nirvana, to redemption. Many Tibetans permanently glide the beads of their rosaries through their fingers, murmuring the mantra: "Om mani padme hum". This prayer collects the spiritual forces and helps to concentrate them in the right direction.

In this connection it is essential to concentrate the spirit on the significance of compassion, the embodiment or emanation of which the Dalai Lama is believed to be. The flowing resonances of the mantra "Om mani padme hum" are meant to generate compassion in the hearts of the faithful.

The sacred art of Tibet, i.e. statues, thangkas and

frescoes, have the sole purpose of serving as an aid to meditation and as inspiration for deeper insight. This is the essence of Mahayana Buddhism.

The traveller who visits Tibet will rapidly realise how much the Tibetans long for the return of their God-king in exile, the Dalai Lama. Hardly a quarter of an hour passes without a foreigner being asked for a picture of the Dalai Lama.

Like the Christian saints in Europe in the early Middle Ages, the saints of Tibet — the Boddhisattvas — are present everywhere. We meet them in the history of Tibet, but also in significant places in the countryside, in the mountains, lakes, and especially of course in the remaining monasteries as well as in the ruins of about 6,000 monasteries destroyed by the Chinese.

The patroness saint of Tibet is the Green Tara. Even Mao Zedong referred to her in a conversation with the Dalai Lama at the beginning of the fifties, and — much to the surprise of the Dalai Lama — suddenly seemed to show genuine respect towards her. The magnificent lake Yamdrok Tso, about 120 kilometers south of Lhasa, to which the Chinese have recently built electric power lines and where an hydro-electric power station is being constructed — a sacrilege which frightens the Tibetans — is under her special protection.

The histories of the Bodhisattvas, Dalai Lamas, Panchen Lamas, Sakya Lamas and other Rinpoches — i.e. reincarnations of Bodhisattvas or saints — are not accounts of sufferings like those of many Christian saints. They are histories of great teachers, who by their merit reached enlightenment, but who declined to enter Nirvana, preferring to help mankind. They remain among men in order to assist them on their way to perfection. Their mortal remains are kept for veneration in gorgeous shrines made of silver and gold, adorned with precious stones in the monasteries, temples and in the Potala palace.

The Bodhisattvas — first among them Avalokiteshvara, emanation of compassion, Manjushri, emanation of wisdom, and Vajrapani, emanation of might and energy — ruled and rule not only over temples and monasteries, but also over the vast land, over towns, villages, roads, routes and mountain paths. Hence they rule in the vastness of space, in which the Potala, the palace of the Dalai Lamas, rises in Lhasa and which is dominated in the west of Tibet by the holy mountain Kailash, throne of the gods and the spiritual centre. Believers pray daily in the temples in front of the sculptures or *thangkas* of the Bodhisattvas. In religious ceremonies, and in meditation on the memory of the salutary deeds of the Bodhisattvas, they evoke the mystic force in which Tibet believes.

Religious Practices

Since a great number of the educated monks were killed by the Chinese, the standard of religious knowledge in Tibet is nowadays not at the same level as it used to be. The religious knowledge is preserved by the Tibetans in exile, especially at the monastic universities in Karnataka, South India, and in Dharamsala, the residence of the Dalai Lama. The full formation of monks in the theological and philosophical teachings takes fifteen to twenty years at Gelugpa universities. The graduate receives the title *geshe*, a kind of PhD. Only then is he allowed to carry out tantric studies and practices.

The formation within the Nyingma and Kagyü orders is different; the monks engage early in tantric practices. Often they follow the way of the Vajrayana and acquire the knowledge needed for this through meditation and yoga.

Vajrayana means the diamond vehicle. As in Mahayana, the objective is not enlightenment for oneself, but for the sake of others. The foundation of Vajrayana are Buddhist tantras, that is the esoteric teachings of Buddha suited to only a select section of the faithful. By practicing Vajrayana, energies are supposed to be activated. The believer attempts to imagine him or herself as a deity, or as a *Yidam*, with the objective of reaching enlightenment. The "clear light", supposed to be visible during this kind of meditation, can normally only be recognised briefly after clinical death.

In Tibet, the importance of the practice of popular beliefs has become even greater than during the period before 1959, given the present lack of qualified teachers and correct spiritual guidance. These practices managed to survive the time of persecution during the Cultural Revolution. The most obvious manifestations of popular religious practices are the recitations of mantras, like "Om mani padme hum", and triple prostrations during which the head touches the ground in front of the statues of Buddha or Bodhisattvas. Of equal importance are clockwise circumambulation of temples and shrines and of donations in the temples, often of liquified butter from the milk of the Dri, the female Yak, for the butter lamps which burn in all temples.

The turning of prayer-mills is supposed to be an invocation of the spirit for the recital of mantras. It is believed to be an act by which the practitioner gains merit. In Nepal, while trekking to the Base Camp of Mount Everest, I saw prayer-mills, painted with vivid colours, on which was written in Tibetan calligraphy: "Om mani padme hum". The energy for turning the wheels was produced by the water power of a torrent. These mechanical prayer-mills are also found in Tibet. I suppose that the purpose of the prayer — to gain merit for better Karma — is not diminished by the mechanical device. The human spirit is indeed inventive.

The word "Lama" means "spiritual or religious leader". The term in Sanskrit is "Guru". The lama is expected to lead his pupils on the path to enlightenment. Padmasambhava, Milarepa and Tsongkhapa are prominent among the important lamas in Tibet's history. They figure on many Thangkas. It is the task of the lama to teach his pupils the most significant ethical principles of the teaching of Mahayana, the great vehicle, on the way to enlightenment: generosity, moral conduct, tolerance, energy, meditation and wisdom.

The four most important sects or orders of Tibetan Buddhism are: Gelugpa, Sakya, Kagyü and Nyingma. The Gelugpa order is also called the order of the Yellow Hats. The Dalai Lama and Panchen Lama belong to the Order of the Yellow Hats. The three other schools figure traditionally as the Order of the Red Hats. This classification is not quite accurate. The differences are more complex and not really a question of the colour of hats. The Nyingma order and its subsidiary orders represent the oldest school of Tibetan Buddhism, based on the ancient translations of tantric Buddhist texts since the seventh century.

Sakya, Kagyü and Gelugpa rely on the so-called new translations, made since the eleventh century.

The remaining major monasteries of Tibet are Sera

and Drepung in Lhasa, Tashilhunpo at Shigatse and the Sakya monastery south of Shigatse. Ganden monastery was completely destroyed, but has since been partly reconstructed. Since the beginning of the eighties relative religious liberty again prevails in Tibet. The Chinese bureaucracy tolerates a very limited number of monks.

However, many security officials and their agents in monastic robes, control the activities of the monks. The traditions of the monasteries continue to live mainly because new monasteries were founded in exile, especially in India, by monks who took refuge after 1959. Hence it was possible to preserve continuity in the education of monks and nuns and the proclamation of the teaching of Buddha, especially the Mahayana rituals.

The Power of Faith as a Source of Strength for Daily Life: Ultimate Aim Nirvana

The strength of faith of the Tibetans relies to a large extent on the veneration of their spiritual and secular ruler in exile, the Dalai Lama. For many Tibetans the Dalai Lama as king and divinity is almighty. It is a concept of the almighty as we conceive it in our childhood, impressed by the absolute certainty of all-embracing justice, goodness and compassion in a king.

The Dalai Lama prefers to see himself as a simple monk. Replying to the question after a lecture in Singapore, at which 5,000 guests attended, as to whether he was a king or a god, he replied: "I am both, I am king and I am God". Then he laughed his cordial and vigorous laughter and added: "No, you know, I am only a humble monk".

33

I questioned many people in Tibet as to their relationship to the Dalai Lama. Almost all Tibetans, whom I met, asked for his photo. I carried only two such photographs of the Dalai Lama and myself during an audience. I had to be cautious, because the distribution of Dalai Lama pictures would constitute a violation of Chinese law. When I nevertheless gave one of the pictures to an old man, his reaction was.moving. With tears in his eyes he took the picture, lifted it high and moved it downwards to touch his forehead. This was a gesture which I observed subsequently many times.

Touching a photograph of the Dalai Lama is supposed — according to general belief – to be a blessing. I was moved in an awkward way when the old men bowed and kissed my hand with an expression of devout veneration, probably in the belief of my special closeness to the Dalai Lama.

Some years ago in the vicinity of Darjeeling in India I met Kalu Rinpoche, a lama, who had meditated in a cave for thirteen years, three months and three days. He was a member of the Kagyü school, founded by Marpa in the eleventh century. The eighty three-year-old lama was venerated like a saint by his followers. When I asked him what could be done for Tibet, he replied: "We can do nothing, it is Karma. I pray for Tibet".

In the historic concept of Buddhists, Karma, i.e. the accumulation of good and evil deeds in the past and their repercussions in the present and future, is not only an individual matter, but an issue which concerns people collectively. Karma, i.e. the balance of good and evil deeds of generations in previous historic epochs, has an inevitable influence on fate in the present and for the future.

And so it was also the comment of a high-ranking

former assistant to the late Panchen Lama, that the only thing which made sense, was to pray for Tibet. The conditions of life for Tibetans were very bad. The Chinese lied incessantly. It was impossible to trust them. The only solution for Tibet would be independence; autonomy alone would lead to nothing. The Chinese had not respected the seventeen-point Agreement of 1951. The most important States in the world, the United States of America and England, on which Tibetans had placed their hopes, had deserted Tibet. They saw only their own interests. Tibet had been independent. But it might have been better in the early forties to allow British troops to enter and to have become a British colony. Hence Tibet would be free today like other British colonies. He had worked a long time for the Panchen Lama, who was not in the position to say everything which he wanted to say. Nevertheless, he was able to reintroduce Tibetan language lessons in schools.

The former American President, Jimmy Carter, had spoken with the Panchen Lama during a visit in Lhasa. Germany's Chancellor Helmut Kohl had also wished to have such a talk when he travelled to Lhasa. The Chinese, however, refused to permit this.

The Tashilhunpo monastery in Shigatse, former residence of the Panchen Lama, now has 900 monks. Peking has limited the number. Now Chinese officials who administer Tibet have to give consent to the ordination of each monk or nun.

At the moment, everywhere in Tibet socialist re-education classes are held. Participants are bound to learn by heart Marxist-Leninist slogans. The main content of the classes — however, is propaganda against the Dalai Lama and disseminating proof that he is a very evil individual.

Tibetans also have to learn, how they should behave towards the "splittists who come from abroad". Classes last up to three weeks; they are designed to encompass the entire population. Nomads are also forced attend and, most importantly, monks and nuns.

In spite of all these efforts even small children are already fervent worshippers of the Dalai Lama.

The reason for this enduring belief of the Tibetans is the powerful personality of the Dalai Lama. Without him the situation would be different.

The Potala palace and the Jokhang temple are being "restored" by the Chinese. This means that at least twenty percent of the well-preserved substance of the buildings is being vandalised, that most of the beautiful frescoes of the Buddhas and Bodhisattvas are being destroyed in order to reconstruct, to modernise and to repaint them. I asked for the background to such destructive renovation. Did the Chinese wish to Sinisize the holiest temple of Tibet? Did they intend to disgrace those most venerated buildings of the Tibetans? The reply, in sad resignation, was that this seemed to be exactly the case.

The Chinese, with their materialistic ideology, appeared to be thrilled to find out what was hidden behind those walls, now destroyed, to learn what constituted the holiness and spiritual strength which finds its resonance in the strong faith of the Tibetans. The destruction of the Potala palace and of the Jokhang are in a way a dissection of the most magnificent architectural manifestations of the spirituality of Tibetans.

But everywhere the hope can be felt that the situation may change soon. Many Tibetans express their opinion that Tibet could be independent within a year — a view which is for Western visitors too optimistic.

I did not know much about the basic fundamental spiritual tenets of Buddhist teaching, particularly regarding the aspiration to reach Nirvana and enlightenment, which is certainly central to the spiritual objectives of all Buddhists.

So, at the end of a meeting with the Dalai Lama in Dharamsala, I asked him as the last of many questions if he could explain to me the concept of enlightenment. The Dalai Lama replied:

"Enlightenment means to know everything".

I ventured to reply: "Only very few people will have this privilege".

The Dalai Lama smiled and continued:

"The nature of mind in itself is something very misleading, because mind consists of sources of interconnected power. Therefore, mind has its limits. So, you see, when the limits of mind is overcome, all organs of sense or the mind are united by the appearing light. I say organs of sense, since much depends on the crude physical. Therefore, the physical energy involved represents a limitation. Thus, you see, the sense of sight is limited to only a certain distance. Compared to this, mind can reach further afield, not depending on the physical organs of sight. So it is more subtle. You see, it can go further. Still this crude mind depends greatly on the physical brain. Therefore, there is still a limitation on it. Thereafter, you see, mind becomes more independent and it becomes more subtle and overcomes all these physical obstacles.

"Then for the mindful nature there is an urge to know, you see, to know. The urge to knowledge is great. Consequently, you see, the physical obstacle is removed. The power of knowing needs no effort to increase. So long as the physical obstacle is removed, the knowing power is there. Thus enlightenment means the state of a complete removal of mental obscuration. So, you see, once the obstacle is removed, the mind becomes all-knowing, I mean knowing everything."

I asked: "Is it possible only for Buddhists to reach this stage, or can Christians or eventually Muslims attain it?"

The Dalai Lama replied:

"Those are religions who believe in... accept the creator. Thus it is a relation of creator and creature. I think, I would say, there are certain variations with the creator, of course, knowing everything, and the creature that the creator created... I don't know... Anyway, when we reach heaven or when we come close to God, then, I think basically we may share some broad knowledge."

HOPE FOR CHANGE

"The teaching of Lord Buddha, and of Jesus, says that universal peace can be achieved by practicing religion. To have one enemy means to increase the number of enemies."

Thupten Phuntsok, Abbot of Nechung Monastery (Seat of the State Oracle of Tibet)

Radiation of Spirit and Will

Jakob Burkhardt 120 years ago in his *Observations on World History*, described what he called "historical crises", which cause the "historical process of the world suddenly to attain frightful speed; developments, which otherwise would take centuries, seem to pass in months and weeks like futile phenomena, and hence appear to be settled." For these patterns he coined the term "overwhelming wind of change".

In his book *We Need Our History* the German essayist Herbert Kremp comments on the contradiction between Spengler's philosophy of history and Toynbee's reflections. He writes: "The cultures of humanity were — according to the British historian — not subjected to the fatal cycle of organic life, but constituted a response of liberty to the challenge of the environment. Their decay was not caused by biological reasons, but resulted from the diminishing radiation of spirit and will. Cultures were not determined or isolated from each other like nomads. From wrecked social systems spiritual and religious movements emerged, being ready to give an epoch-making response to the challenge of their time. The new developments emerged from struggles and sacrifices. One ought to be in the position to recognise this from the course of history."

Furthermore Herbert Kremp points out: "The spiritual nature of man can be ruled, as in physical science, by the law of *horror vacui*; then, at certain times, something pours in, which imperiously demands faith."

Apparently Mao Zedong was very well aware that the structures and the new society of the People's Republic created by him and the Communist Party of China also bore the stigma of transitoriness. A remark to which the German author Peter Scholl-Latour refers in his book, *The Illusion of Heavenly Peace*, published in 1990, is attributed to Mao Zedong: "I am only a poor monk beneath an umbrella perforated by holes." This remark seems to reflect a fundamental Taoist-Buddhist conviction.

We can take it as granted that thought structures and behaviour patterns in China continue to be under the influence of the great religions and philosophical ideas of the Middle Kingdom, not only of Buddhism, but also of Taoism and of the teachings of Confucius. Hence there is a relation between religion and politics.

In his first autobiography the Dalai Lama reminisces on an encounter with Mao Zedong. Mao said: "Tibet is a big country. You have a wonderful history. A long time ago you conquered even a huge part of China. But now you have fallen back, and we want to help you. After twenty years you will have surpassed us, and then it will be your turn to help us. "The Dalai Lama could hardly believe what he had just heard. Nevertheless, he thought that Mao Zedong had said this out of conviction and not out of cheap showmanship.

If we consider the situation of China and Tibet today, not twenty, but more than forty years after the prediction of Mao Zedong, Mao seems to have been right, at least concerning the need for spiritual help for China given the vacuum caused by the failure of Marxism-Leninism and Mao Zedong Thought.

I became intrigued by the analysis of epochal transformations and political changes, and I tried to investigate the respective causes further. I was mainly interested in gaining greater knowledge about the possible influence of Tibetan Buddhism on the future political development of China on which, in turn, Tibet's fate will depend.

Nostalgia for Freedom and Cosmological Providence

According to the Tibetan philosophical concept of history its course is determined by cosmological forces. Karma is supposed to be the decisive force in the course of affairs, i.e. the weighing up of good and evil deeds, not only of individuals, but also of peoples through epochs.

The sudden liberation of a country after dozens of years of oppression must appear to us like a miracle — as Vaclav Havel, President of Czechoslovakia, said of his country after the transition. To religious people in the West it may seem to be the grace of God, to Buddhists a cosmological providence resulting from the accumulation of good Karma.

The Far Eastern Economic Review reported that several participants in the demonstrations on Tiananmen Square in Peking in May and early June 1989, shortly before the cruel massacres committed by the Chinese People's Liberation Army, performed very ancient Mahayana Buddhist rituals which once were common on the occasion of sacrifices.

Tibetan authors refer in their volume *Tibet, the Facts* to an interesting thesis whereby the demonstrations of the students on Tiananmen Square against the brutal actions and the use of guns by the Chinese police in Lhasa, and the subsequent extensive reporting of events in the Chinese media, seem to have created a kind of triggering element.

This led to the creation of an excited and critical consciousness among various Chinese students and other demonstrators. This consciousness may have contributed to an increasingly critical attitude among the

Chinese and to their readiness to act.

Did the spirit of Tiananmen have repercussions on the liberation movement in Eastern Europe? Are there analogies in the modes of behaviour?

Participants in the demonstrations in Leipzig in October and November 1989, which triggered the collapse of Honecker's regime, reported feeling an "inner compulsion", which moved them to travel long distances, often from remote areas of the Saxonian province, to take part in the protests. They came in spite of the imminent danger that the security forces could open fire on them, following the example of the massacre in Tiananmen Square in Peking in June 1989, which had been praised by the leadership of the GDR. Parents, who joined the demonstrations, left their children behind, uncertain, if they ever would see them again.

The nostalgia for liberty, this essential right of each man, seems to continue to be at work. After the breaking-up of the Soviet Union and Yugoslavia, the cohesion of which was based on force, more and more territories everywhere in the world aspire to self-determination, autonomy, or independence. Values are involved, good and evil have a significance.

In regions which aspire to freedom, spiritual guidance in politics is of special importance for setting the course. In the enthusiasm for newly achieved liberty, however, excessively euphoric assessments or exaggerations can also emerge. Hence, certain Western schools of thought reach very different conclusions as compared to the Buddhist history of philosophy. Francis Fukuyama, the former deputy chief of the Planning Section in the American State Department, announced in 1990 that he considered the final victory of liberal democracy marked the "end of history". In his view we

43

are now experiencing not only the end of the Cold War, or the termination of a specific period of Post-War history, but the end of history itself: this means the final destination of the ideological development of human-kind and the universal rule of Western liberal democracy as the final form of government of men.

This statement seems to reflect extraordinary optimism. It is questionable, however, if it is farsighted. Fukuyama's view relies exclusively on a Western, Eurocentric approach, closely linked to the German philosopher of the first half of the nineteenth century, Georg Friedrich Hegel.

In reality, world history, however, is likely to be much more complex than could have been predicted 160 years ago. By all means, it appears to be useful to take into consideration not only European schools of thought, which are conditioned by Cartesian thinking, but also Eastern schools of thought, mainly Buddhist philosophy. One of the main principles of Buddhist philosophy consists in the awareness that everything is constantly changing. This corresponds to the *panta rhei* (everything is flowing) of Greek philosophy. Scepticism should therefore reign, if we talk today of the end of history, even if the Western system of liberal democracy seems to be triumphing everywhere in the world and is considered also by oppressed people — including Tibetans and the Dalai Lama himself — as the "best" system of government.

I asked the Dalai Lama if, according to Buddhist teaching, the idea of the possibility of unexpected political changes caused by a kind of cosmological providence, similar to the concept of divine mercy, existed. The Dalai Lama replied:

"Yes, there are such indications. Anyway, the darkest period for Tibet is over. At the moment, however, the restrictions for the people have become even more severe."

A few lines from the autobiography of the Dalai Lama clearly determine the sources of power underlying the nostalgia for liberty.

"We all seek happiness and try to avoid suffering. We have the same basic needs and concerns. Furthermore, all of us human beings want freedom and the right to determine our own destiny as individuals. That is human nature. The great changes taking place everywhere in the world, from Eastern Europe to Africa, are a clear indication of this."

Strategies for Change

The Dalai Lama then replied to my question concerning a strategy to influence the thoughts and ideas of the current and future leaders in China:

"I believe that there will be a change in the next five to ten years in China. Some of the Chinese student leaders, who now live in free countries, have exactly the same opinion. Certainly, the present situation, which is determined by the thinking of the hard-liners, will be due for a change. All countries of Eastern Europe have completely changed. Russia itself is in a very rapid process of change. So also China, a very big country, which is in a difficult situation, will not be able to elude change."

As to my question concerning values which might be able to fill the vacuum, which also exists in China because of the crisis of Marxism-Leninism, the Dalai Lama replied:

"At the moment there is great confusion for thousands upon thousands of Chinese youths. Their ambition is concentrated especially on earning more money and to becoming rich. Once those needs have been more or less satisfied, they will certainly realise that something is missing. Only a short time ago they believed that communism meant everything. Now this ideology has broken down completely. China's youth has lost its belief in communism. Therefore another ideology, which is not yet present, will come and remain."

Finally, he said in respect to the future role of Buddhism in China: "For many centuries Buddhism had great influence in China. Therefore it will be in a position to easily gain strength again."

He mentioned that the predecessor to the Tenth Panchen Lama, who died in 1989, had presided over a Kalachakra Initiation ceremony in Peking. If he himself were to do the same this would not constitute a precedent. His care and his efforts as a Buddhist monk encompassed all human beings, indeed all sentient beings. All human beings desired freedom, and the right to determine as individuals their own fate. In 1953 the Dalai Lama received from his teacher, Ling Rinpoche, the Kalachakra Initiation, which is one of the most important tantric initiations. The Tibetans believe in its importance for world peace. It is carried out in front of a large number of believers. For this purpose a huge Mandala has to be formed from coloured grains of sand. Its significance is due to the fact that, though bi-dimensional, it represents a tri-dimensional symbol. The Dalai Lama writes in his autobiography that he was especially moved himself during the initiation ceremony. Later he considered this as an auspicious sign and as an augur that he would indeed preside over more Kalachakra ceremonies than each of his predecessors, and this everywhere in the world. By the summer of 1995 he had already performed nineteen such Kalachakra Initiations.

Tibet's Oracle of State and the Influence of Religion on Politics

The seat of the Oracle of State, Nechung monastery in Dharamsala, is the centre of the teaching of Abidharmakosa, i.e. the cosmology of metaphysics. The literal translation is: *Treasure House of the Special Teaching.*

The original Nechung monastery is situated close to Lhasa in Tibet. A new monastery was built in Dharamsala, following the flight of the Dalai Lama from Tibet.

The Abbot, Thupten Phuntsok Rinpoche, told me that the Chinese had claimed that they succeeded in completely destroying the Nechung monastery in Lhasa. At that time it proved difficult to get reliable news from Tibet and the Tibetans therefore built a new Nechung monastery in Dharamsala. The rituals of the monastery have a special meaning and are mainly from the Nyingma tradition. Many monks of Christian orders come to study the rituals.

The Abbot explained to me the meaning of the State Oracle for the Tibetans. In the Oracle, Dhammapala, the protector of religion, manifests himself and it is possible to consult the Oracle as to dharma-practices (Dharma = Buddhist teaching) and over religious questions. The Oracle existed for the faithful. Religious and political questions were often mixed; they were not independent from each other. Hence the predictions of the Oracle also had an influence on political matters.

The Abbot replied to my question concerning the influence of religion on politics in Tibet:

"The Buddhist teaching has great influence in politics. The fundamental idea is to enhance the condition of happiness and to avoid the condition of unhappiness. To achieve happiness, good deeds have to be accomplished; good deeds have to accumulate. As everybody tries to strive for happiness, the Chinese too aspire to happiness. Even if the Chinese humiliate the Tibetans, the Tibetans have the desire to help the Chinese. The Chinese did not create good Karma; the result of their actions is negative. The fight between Tibetans and Chinese continues, not because the Chinese have bad qualities, but because they pursue a very bad policy against the Tibetans. The Buddhist teaching shows us the right behaviour.

"The Chinese do not respect the Ten Commandments. In East Germany the same problem existed. People had to obey the commandments of communism. World peace can only be achieved through religion. Even the slightest norm of conduct is stipulated by religion. The inhabitants of the GDR had a clear vision of their happiness; they wanted to achieve it. As a result of these aspirations a peaceful world can be created.

The teachings of Buddha, of Jesus, say that by practicing religion universal peace can be achieved. To have an enemy means to increase the number of enemies. If the Chinese had killed me, I would not really have been killed, only my external body. If I am killed by Chinese hands, and if I am reborn, the same feeling of hatred would continue to exist.

48

"The Panchen Lama died in 1989. We all believe that he will be reincarnated. We all know that in the next Panchen Lama the same feeling towards the Chinese will continue. After the torture of a prisoner, his spirit and his fundamental attitude will remain the same if the prisoner does not want it otherwise. Religion is the most important means to control spirit and fundamental attitude.

"The State Oracle says that there will be negative consequences if men continually commit demeritorious actions, but that good Karma can be achieved if they accumulate good actions.

"The difference between the populations of Tibet and China is comparable to that between an ant and an elephant. The Chinese will have to leave silently. The Tibetans have the truth. In 1959 the Chinese said that India and China were brothers; in 1962 they attacked India. Today, concerning the question of Tibet, all nations are against China."

Demonstration against China, 1985.

CHINA'S POLICY TOWARDS TIBET

"From west to east, clouds drift in the sky,
My garment is full of stains;
The clouds will vanish,
The stains will remain."
 Tibetan folk song

A Battle is Lost

When Mao Zedong received a report on the revolt of March 1959 in Lhasa, in which it was stated that order had been restored, he asked about the fate of the Dalai Lama. When he was informed that he had succeeded in escaping, he exclaimed: "In this case, we have lost a battle."

Travellers over the Khunjerab Pass, from Pakistan into Chinese Sinkiang, receive booklets about Tibet from an official Chinese information office at the border entitled: *Freedom of Religious Belief in Tibet, The Dalai Lama and the Seventeen-Article-Agreement, Numbers and Facts Concerning the Population of Tibet, Figures and Facts on the Population of Tibet and Old, but Vigorous Country on the Roof of the World* The last brochure shows a photograph of the Chancellor of the Federal Republic of Germany, Helmut Kohl, and his wife during a visit to Lhasa in 1987.

The authors of these brochures go a long way back in history to justify the Chinese position that Tibet is part of China. In the year 641 A.D. the Chinese princess Wencheng of the Tang Dynasty married the Tibetan king Songtsan Gampo. It is claimed that when she arrived in Tibet, she brought a statue of the Buddha Shakyamuni and a collection of Buddhist scripts as well as artists and artisans. Those presents are supposed to have been an important contribution to the development of Tibetan culture.

The authors of the Chinese propaganda brochures claim that later, when another Chinese princess, Jincheng, married the Tibetan leader Tride Tsugden, relations between the Han (i.e. the Chinese) and the Tibetans became increasingly close.

Since 1264, when Emperor Kublai Khan appointed the Tibetan Phagpa as "royal advisor" and entrusted him with the responsibility for Tibet's religious affairs, close relations between religion and politics have existed. Later Chinese governments during the Yuan, Ming and Qing dynasties followed the example of Kublai Khan by installing Buddhist leaders as the most effective form of government in Tibet. For 700 years, therefore, political and religious authority has been in the same hands.

One pamphlet depicts a mural painting in the Sakya monastery in Tibet in which the Dalai Lama can be seen during his visit to the Emperor Shunzhi in Peking in 1652.

The argument continues by claiming that through the close relationship between secular and religious rule, Buddhism lost purity, and excesses— such as the serfdom of hundreds of thousands occurred.

Only the "peaceful liberation" of 1951 and the "democratic reforms" of 1959 had finally brought real freedom to Tibet by breaking the old system and opening a new epoch.

In the brochure *Freedom of Religious Belief in Tibet* it is said: "It cannot be denied that the religious policy in Tibet, as in other regions of the country, was destroyed by the Cultural Revolution(1966-1976). After this turbulence the Communist Party of China and the Chinese government gradually corrected the mistake and took several measures, including the liberty of religious belief. At the moment, there are 1,400 monasteries and places for religious activities, ca. 34,000 lamas and nuns, a number which should correspond more or less to the normal religious needs of the monastic and secular masses."

53

Unfortunately, the number of monasteries, monks and nuns is highly exaggerated. There are no more than several hundred monasteries and several thousand monks and nuns.

Before 1959, 114,000 monks and nuns lived in 2,700 monasteries and temples. After the "democratic reforms" this number was reduced to 6,900 monks in 550 monasteries. After the turmoil of the Cultural Revolution between 1966 and 1976, only eight monasteries with 970 monks and nuns were left.

In another pamphlet: *The Dalai Lama and the Seventeen-Article Agreement*, an attempt is made via a historical misinterpretation to pretend that the Dalai Lama agreed in 1951 to the Seventeen-Article Agreement, in which the sovereignty of Tibet is abandoned. This alleged consent, however, was reached by force. The Dalai Lama told me in this respect:

"Because of the Seventeen-Article Agreement of 1951, which was not signed voluntarily, but under force, China was able to annex Tibet. There are similarities between the annexation of the Baltic States and that of Tibet."

At the end of the Cultural Revolution, and after the death of Mao Zedong, Chinese policy in Tibet improved with the gradual rise to power of Deng Xiaoping since the end of the seventies, and in the early eighties. Hu Yaobang visited Tibet. Soon the local officials were afraid of him, because he never let his daily programme be known in advance, but arrived to inspect the various authorities in Lhasa and in the provinces without previous announcement. Hu Yaobang expressed his amazement about living conditions in Lhasa and asked if the huge quantities of money which had been so far received had been thrown into the river. Furthermore, he promised an eighty five percent reduction of Chinese personnel stationed in Tibet. As the Dalai Lama mentions in his autobiography, later on little was heard about these measures. Hu Yaobang's rise to the hierarchy of the powerful soon ended, and he was forced to resign from his post as Secretary-General of the Communist Party. He was met with reproaches because of his "lax" policy, which was supposed to have caused the student demonstrations of December 1986 in China.

The Dalai Lama remembers to this day with gratitude the deceased statesman because of his courage in admitting the mistakes of the Chinese leadership in Tibet.

Besides Hu Yaobang, Vice-Prime Minister Wan Li was mainly responsible for the brief but positive change in China's policies towards Tibet. In 1980 he had accompanied Hu Yaobang at his visit to Tibet. In 1984 the politicians Hu Qili and Tian Jiyun, proteges of Hu Yaobang and Prime Minister Zhao Ziyang, visited Tibet and confirmed China's new Tibet policy.

One year earlier, in 1983, a delegation of the Circle of Christian Democratic Students from Germany, presided over by the former Chairman of this body, Johannes Weberling, arrived in Peking, invited by the All-Chinese Student Association.

I had the opportunity to talk to members of the delegation in Singapore, where they stayed during a stopover on their journey to Peking, and to brief them on the principal concern of the Dalai Lama, respect for human rights in Tibet. Indeed, the delegation raised this concern in Peking. The newspaper *China Reconstructs* in August 1983 printed an interview with Johannes Weberling:

"Q: What are your experiences concerning China's minority policy?

"A: As you may perhaps recall, eleven or twelve years ago we criticized conditions in a relatively harsh way, mainly those in Tibet... Also the Secretary-General of the CCP has admitted that in Tibet many mistakes have been committed, and that something has to be done to correct these mistakes.On our journey to China we talked to some Tibetans who told us that something has changed positively. Now it is again possible in China to pursue religious activities, which was not possible before..."

Hence, it is likely that in 1983 a strong lobby in favour of Tibet existed within the Chinese Government. Otherwise even the printing of these lines in an official Chinese publication would have been impossible.

There have been, and there still are at present, thousands of political prisoners in Chinese prisons. From these prisons day after day the melody of an old Tibetan folk song can be heard:

"From west to east, clouds drift in the sky,

My garment is full of stains;

The clouds will vanish,

The stains will remain."

The Chinese did and do not understand the "subversive" content of this melody. "The clouds will vanish"; by the clouds disappearing towards the east, the Chinese themselves are meant. Contrary to the announcement of Hu Yaobang that eighty five percent of the Chinese officials would be withdrawn from Tibet, a period of massive Chinese settlement began in Tibet in 1984.

The Chinese policy of settlement has already achieved a situation whereby today the circa 7.5 million Chinese in Tibet constitute a majority as compared to the 6 million Tibetans. According to Chinese statistics, there are now 2.5 million Chinese in Amdo province and only 450,000 Tibetans.

With contempt for mankind, the brutal colonial policy of Peking — which culminates in the systematic violation of fourteen and fifteen year old girls by Chinese officers, in medical experiments leading to the death of Tibetan patients, as well as in the sterilisation of all Tibetan women able to give birth who can be reached— has led since 1987 to new revolts which have been quelled with bloodshed.

The Role of the Panchen Lama

Both the First Dalai Lama and the First Panchen Lama were pupils of Tsongkhapa, founder of the Gelugpa school of Buddhism. The first recognised Panchen Lama incarnation was Lobsang Chokyi Gyaltsen (1570-1662). In the seventeenth century the V Dalai Lama recognised the Panchen Lama as a reincarnation of Amitabha, the Buddha of Limitless Light. In the early eighteenth century the Manchus, who had deposed the VII Dalai Lama, offered the Panchen Lama control over extended areas of Tibet — an offer which he, however, declined.

There are contradicting views concerning the former position of the X Panchen Lama in Tibet and about his role until his death in 1989.

The following account is a summary of information provided by Kalon Tripa Sonam Topgyal, who then held the position of Secretary-General of the Departmemt of Information and International Relations of the Tibetan Government-in-Exile in Dharamsala.

The Panchen Lama was born in 1938 in the village of Karang Bidho in Amdo province in Eastern Tibet. The

Chinese Government tried throughout his life — beginning already during the rule of the Kuomintang — to use him for its own ends, and especially to use him to weaken the authority of the Dalai Lama and his Government.

The Panchen Lama ranked after the Dalai Lama as the second highest dignitary in Tibet. His seat was Tashilhunpo monastery in Shigatse, Central Tibet.

I questioned Tibetans in Lhasa and Shigatse. They concurred in expressing the opinion that the spiritual and secular authority of the Dalai Lama in Tibet had been even further strengthened by the death of the Panchen Lama.

At the beginning of this century the Chinese succeeded in creating a rift between the then XIII Dalai Lama and the IX Panchen Lama: Antagonism existed because of taxes which had to be paid by people living within the territory of the Panchen Lama to the government of the Dalai Lama. Officials of the Panchen Lama asked Peking for help and the Tibetan Government in Lhasa sent troops to Shigatse. The Panchen Lama then fled to China. The Chinese tried to win advantages from this fact. They impeded the return of the Panchen Lama to his home. He died in 1937 in a monastery in Kham. In 1941 officials, who had fled earlier with the Panchen Lama to China, selected from three possible reincarnations the three-year-old Gonpo Tseten as the X Panchen Lama. This was a violation of the prerogative of the Dalai Lama or respectively his regent and the Tibetan National Assembly, to decide about the selection of the Panchen Lama. In 1949 the reincarnation was recognised by Tsung-ren, the then acting President of China.

In 1949, the commander of Chinese forces in Lanzhou initiated contact with the eleven-year-old Panchen Lama under orders from Mao Zedong. On 1st October 1949, the day the People's Republic of China was proclaimed, he was forced to send a telegram to Mao Zedong asking him for the "liberation" of Tibet. Mao Zedong replied: "The Tibetan people feel great love for the motherland. It refutes the foreign imperialists and is prepared to join the new, united, egalitarian and powerful People's Republic of China."

At this time the Panchen Lama was neither recognised by the government of Tibet nor had he any spiritual or political authority in Tibet.

After 1951, Mao Zedong cultivated a close relationship with the Panchen Lama, who lived in Peking. At this time the Dalai Lama recognised the Panchen Lama as the reincarnation of the late IX Panchen Lama, following a request from representatives of Tashilhunpo monastery. He received the title Tenzin Trinley Jigme Choe-kyi Wangchuk.

In April 1952, the Panchen Lama arrived in Lhasa and was greeted there as well as in the three monasteries Sera, Drepung, and Ganden with great enthusiasm by masses of people.

In 1956, the Panchen Lama was appointed by the Chinese as Deputy-Chairman of the Preparatory Committee of the "Autonomous Region of Tibet". The Dalai Lama became Chairman. After the flight of the Dalai Lama to India in 1959 the Chinese appointed the Panchen Lama as "acting Chairman". One year later, he became Deputy-Chairman of the National People's Congress of China. At this time, there were huge waves of detentions in Tibet: China enforced her "reforms".

In consideration of the persecution of many of his compatriots, and of the outrages for which the Chinese Government was responsible, the Panchen Lama sent a petition with 70,000 characters to Premier Zhou Enlai in 1962. The Chinese leader replied that he was happy about his courage and his openness, also if there were mistakes in the wording. He promised that some of the points raised in the petition would be complied with.

In 1964 the Panchen Lama had to undergo severe criticism during the Seventh Session of the Preparatory Committee of the Autonomous Region of Tibet. He was accused of being against the party, socialism and the people, and lost his post as Chairman of the Committee. In Peking he was put under house-arrest until 1965. He had to spend ten years in prison where he was also tortured. With the beginning of the Cultural Revolution he had to take part in many *Thamzing* — public "struggle" sessions of self-accusation, during which he was humiliated and beaten.

In 1980 he was reinstated as the Deputy-Chairman of the National People's Congress of China. Only in 1982 was he allowed to visit Tibet again. Seven further visits followed before his death. The Panchen Lama avoided open criticism against China and tried to do as much as possible for Tibet. It is believed that only thanks to his efforts could Tibetan be taught at schools in Tibet again.

The Dalai Lama mentions in his autobiography that they were able to have a long telephone conversation when the Panchen Lama was in Australia in 1986. He considered the Panchen Lama as a great patriot.

On 28 March 1987 the Panchen Lama made a speech to the "Permanent Committee of the National People's Congress", which was kept secret and only available to the highest cadres of the Communist Party of China. The Government-in-Exile of the Dalai Lama managed to receive a copy. The text has since been published in

English by the information office of the Tibetan Government in Exile. (See Annex I)

In his secret speech the Panchen Lama denounces the systematically planned genocide of Tibetans by the Chinese Government. Significant in this respect is his description of indiscriminate massacres by the Chinese among the civil population – not of participants in uprisings of the 1960s. The only purpose behind this strategy can have been to intimidate the civilians in general and to make them submissive.

According to the Panchen Lama, the attempts of the Chinese Government to ridicule the Tibetan religion and Tibetan convictions leaves a feeling of sadness. For example the presentation of awards to a film *Compassion Without Mercy*, a game with words in which, apparently, an attempt is made to ridicule the Dalai Lama, reincarnation of the deity of compassion or mercy.

The Panchen Lama attempted first to yield in his speech, pretending to be in general agreement with Chinese policy. Then, however, he accounts step-by-step for the crimes of the Chinese occupying forces. He proved much courage with this speech.

In January 1989, the Panchen Lama died during a visit to Tashilhunpo monastery in Shigatse, after having again sharply criticised the Chinese Government because of its policy in Tibet. He had remarked that the price which Tibet had paid for its development in the last thirty years was higher than the gains and that leftist mistakes had caused greater damage than rightist mistakes.

Many Tibetans believe that the Panchen Lama was poisoned. There are, however, also reports of an infarction and of serious efforts by a team of Chinese doctors to save him.

In May 1995 the Dalai Lama recognised a six-year-old Tibetan boy, Gedhun Choekyi Nyima, from Nagchu in Lhari district of Tibet as the reincarnation of the X Panchen Lama. The reaction of the Chinese Government was amazing. Though still officially relying on the Marxist-Leninist Mao-Zedong-thought ideology — and hence a hundred percent secular in its persuasions — Peking claimed it to be its prerogative as it was once the prerogative of the Manchurian emperors, to select the second highest figure of the Tibetan clergy, the Panchen Lama. Events ironically almost paralleled the antagonism between the Emperors of the Holy Roman Empire and the Popes in the eleventh century on the question of investiture, i.e. the prerogative of the selection of bishops, which culminated in the fight between Emperor Henry IV and Pope Gregor VII and finally led to the Emperor falling to his knees in Canossa and asking the Pope for pardon.

The Chinese Government demonstrated considerable nervousness, only because the Dalai Lama announced his official recognition of the reincarnation shortly before the Chinese Government intended to give its approval. The Chinese had gathered that the committee of monks of Shigatse, chaired by the abbot, Chatral Rinpoche, which identified the six-year-old boy who met al! requirements, had made its selection in full loyalty to the Chinese Government. The sudden realisation of the blessing of the Dalai Lama for the choice of the selection committee greatly angered the Chinese. The abbot and many monks of Shigatse were arrested and the XI Panchen Lama simply disappeared. He is believed to be in Peking; no precise information was, however, available on his whereabouts ten months after his detention in July 1995.

In early November 1995 China arranged for rites to identify its choice of reincarnation of the Panchen Lama. Ironically enough, only forty four years earlier, in May 1951, the Chinese Government had insisted that the XIV Dalai Lama himself recognised the X Panchen Lama — who was in their custody — as the reincarnation of the IX Panchen Lama.

A meeting in Peking, at which seventy five cadres and religious figures of Tashilhunpo monastery had been ordered to attend, ended on 11 November 1995 with the endorsement of three Chinese candidates for the reincarnation.

On 29 November 1996, the Chinese authorities chose, by drawing lots, six-year-old Cyaincain Norbu also from Nagchu, northern Tibet, born 13 February 1990, as the XI Panchen Lama. The Chinese ignored that lot-drawing, while within Tibetan tradition, was only rarely used and then as the last resort for determining a true incarnation. Hence, in this exercise, Tibetan religious belief and tradition was disparaged.

Strangely enough, the Chinese Government announced — in deviation from its traditional atheist policies — that at the birth of their choice for the XI Panchen Lama, six years before, auspicious signs, dreams and discoveries were reported. The mother of the fake Panchen Lama was supposed — according to the Hongkong pro-China newspaper *Tao Kung Pao* — to have been visited by Palden Lhamo, the most widely-worshipped female guardian deity of Tibet.

Silence between China and Tibet

Following overtures by the Chinese leadership, and thanks to the initial mediation of the British ambassador in Peking, first contacts between the government of Deng Xiaoping and the Dalai Lama were established in the late 1970s.

Peking facilitated the visits to Tibet of three delegations of the Dalai Lama. The emissaries of the God-king were welcomed in Tibet with overwhelming enthusiasm — much to the chagrin of Peking, which had been convinced of its hold over Tibet.

In 1982, the Chinese Government announced its readiness to facilitate the return of the Dalai Lama. The conditions were laid down in various points. Point Four says:

"The Dalai Lama will enjoy the same political status and living conditions as he had before 1959. It is suggested that he need not go to live in Tibet or hold local posts there. Of course, he may go back to Tibet from time to time. His followers need not worry about their jobs and living conditions. These will only be better than before."

The Dalai Lama was not interested in the question of his own status and privileges. For him, Tibet and the Tibetans mattered.

In 1985, ninety one members of the United States Congress wrote to Li Xiannian, Chairman of the People's Congress in Peking, and favoured direct talks between the Chinese Government and representatives of the Dalai Lama. In this letter the Chinese are asked to meet the "reasonable and justified aspirations of the Dalai Lama and his people".

On 21 September 1987 the Dalai Lama announced

during his speech in Capitol Hill in Washington D.C. the so-called Five Point Peace Plan for Tibet. He asked for:

1. The transformation of the whole of Tibet into a zone of peace.
2. Abandonment of China's population transfer policy which threatens the very existence of the Tibetans as a people.
3. Respect for the Tibetan people's fundamental human rights and democratic freedoms.
4. Restoration and protection of Tibet's natural environment and the abandonment of China's use of Tibet for the production of nuclear weapons and dumping of nuclear waste.
5. Commencement of earnest negotiations on the future status of Tibet and of relations between Tibetan and Chinese peoples.

Since the middle of the eighties the Dalai Lama had realised that the Chinese Government was pursuing a policy of Sinicization which has been called by some commentators the Chinese "Endlösung" for Tibet.

The Dalai Lama writes in his autobiography in respect of his initiatives towards China:

"In my call for negotiations on the future status of Tibet, I expressed my wish to approach the subject in a spirit of frankness and conciliation, with a view to finding a solution that is in the long-term interest of everyone..."

After a speech by the Dalai Lama to the European Parliament in June 1988, China seemed to be ready for a compromise. The Dalai Lama had made concessions and asked only for the full autonomy of Tibet, while he consented that Peking should keep its responsibility for the foreign affairs and defence of Tibet. In autumn

1988, Peking announced itself ready to discuss the future of Tibet with the Dalai Lama. This offer differed from previous offers only in respect of the fact that those had only offered to discuss the "status of the Dalai Lama", not the status of Tibet.

The Dalai Lama appointed an authorised delegation for the negotiations. The negotiations were supposed to begin in January 1989 in Geneva. The Chinese raised ever-new objections, also against the composition of the delegation of the Dalai Lama: They objected that a non-Tibetan, the Dutch M. van Walt van Praag, legal advisor to the Dalai Lama, was included in the Tibetan Delegation. Peking did not seem to be earnestly interested in the negotiations. Indeed there were no talks.

In early summer 1992, Peking approached Gyalo Thondup, an elder brother of the Dalai Lama, who lived in Hongkong and tried to win him to so-called new proposals concerning Tibet. It seemed at first as if China was trying to gain advantage by supporting Thondup and by dividing the family of the Dalai Lama.

On this occasion the Chinese insisted that all details of the talks ought to remain secret. In August 1992 the brother of the Dalai Lama announced in the form of a ten-point declaration in Dharamsala the Chinese proposals to the Tibetan Parliament.

The proposals were essentially meant to grant Tibet autonomy not, however, the independence demanded by Tibetans.

An invitation to a delegation of the Dalai Lama for talks in Peking was expected.

Unfortunately there are many indications that the whole occurrence was no more than a manoeuvre by the Chinese to distract world attention from their colonial policies and violations of human rights.

The Dalai Lama mentioned in his address on the occasion of the 35th anniversary of the Tibetan Uprising Day on March 1994 that he has left no stone unturned in his attempts to reach an understanding with the Chinese. He also mentioned that the Tibetans had placed their hopes on international support and help bringing about meaningful negotiations, to which he still remained committed. If this failed, he would no longer be able to pursue this policy with a clear conscience. He stated that he felt strongly that it would then be his responsibility to consult the people on the future course of the freedom struggle. Just as the late Indian Prime Minister, Jawaharlal Nehru, stated in the Indian Parliament on 7 December 1950, he too had always maintained that the final voice with regard to Tibet should be the Tibetan people.

Desperation among Tibetans about the impasse concerning their fate and the future of their country led to new ventures. In late 1994 and early 1995 a peace-march of five hundred to seven hundred Tibetans from Dharamsala across the Himalayas to Lhasa was under consideration. Serious concerns were raised in respect to such a desperate move which may have ended in a massacre of hundreds of marchers by the hands of Chinese soldiers stationed in Tibet. The Dalai Lama recommended that the peace-march be rerouted into a march from Dharamsala to Delhi.

Escalation of Violence

In September 1987, the Chinese reacted to the announcement of the Five-Point-Peace-Plan by the Dalai Lama in Washington D.C. by show trials and two public executions in Tibet. Thereupon demonstrations occurred in Lhasa. Military and police used their firearms and shot into the crowd. This resulted in dead and wounded. There are videos of these events which were filmed furtively and taken out of Tibet.

In March 1988, Chinese policemen attacked the Jokhang temple and murdered at least twelve monks. The eyes of one of the monks were torn out before he was thrown down from the roof. Then Tibetans burned down about twenty Chinese shops in Lhasa.

On 5 March 1989, again demonstrations against Chinese occurred in Lhasa. Tens of thousands of Tibetans took to the streets. On the first day, the Chinese only took pictures with video cameras, on the next day they shot into the crowd. At least 250 Tibetans died and many were injured. The USA, France, and the European Parliament condemned the action of China.

On 8 March 1989, Peking imposed martial law on Tibet. Only a few weeks after these actions in Lhasa the upheaval in China started, culminating in the tragedy of the massacre on Tiananmen Square.

The Dalai Lama considers that the suppression of the movement for democracy in June 1989 on the Tiananmen Square was only partly successful. He believes that, by its brutal action the Chinese Government created an attitude among the population which favoured the students and their political objectives.

In the autumn of the same year the Dalai Lama received the Nobel Prize for Peace.

In 1991, on the occasion of the fortieth anniversary of the "liberation" of Tibet, the Chinese presented a memorial to the Tibetan people at a Lhasa crossroads. It consists of yaks cast in bronze. "That is the only non-political monument which our liberators could build here, a young Tibetan told me.

At the end of February 1992, a monk was found dead in his cell in the Jokhang temple in Lhasa. He had been strangled with a rope. He was not just an unknown monk. Jampa Tenzin, supervisor of the Jokhang temple, had earlier suffered severe burns during the demonstration for independence of Tibet on 1 October 1987. That day thirty two Tibetans were shot by the Chinese police. A photograph, showing him leading the outraged crowd, went around the world.

After the murder, monks of the Jokhang temple were forced by the police to sign a declaration according to which the case was suicide. Only a few days before the murder, the monks in neighbouring cells are reported to have received an order from the police to change to other more distant cells. On the evening before his assassination policemen came to Lama Jampa Tenzin's cell to interrogate him.

Briefly after the murder of Jampa Tenzin demonstrations by monks from Sera, Drepung and the Jokhang temple started. The demonstrations took place in front of the Jokhang. Each time three to four monks took part, demanding liberty for Tibet. The monks were taken prisoner day after day by the Chinese security forces.

The area around the Jokhang was then declared temporarily off limits. When I visited this prohibited zone in May 1992 I was the only foreigner.

In front of Sera monastery monks had fixed placards which were rapidly removed by the police. On these placards was the message that the monks would continue to demonstrate until Tibet is free. They did not mind if the police emptied the monastery by their arrests. Even the monks who were released from prison would continue to demonstrate.

In Lhasa, already 650 monks and forty nuns had been arrested at that time. Nobody knew their exact number. There are no regular judicial procedures. There is torture in the prisons.

Rumours spread that in the meantime there was no room left in Lhasa's prisons for common criminals because political prisoners occupied all the cells. Hence crime, theft and robbery increased.

"The Chinese are afraid of the monks" many voices in Lhasa whispered.

Violation of Human Rights in Tibet

Practically all visitors who leave Tibet, leave it with a feeling of sadness. Human rights are violated in many respects: It is not possible to take pictures or written teachings of the Dalai Lama to Tibet. The right to freedom of information is violated. Chinese officers are not allowed to pray in Buddhist temples. Otherwise they would be in danger of being expelled from the army. This means that the liberty of religion is not granted. These, however, are only some of the less severe violations.

The Dalai Lama had asked me during a visit to Dharamsala in 1991 to prolong my stay to speak to a young Tibetan, the fate of whom was especially tragic. The office of the Dalai Lama arranged the meeting. I asked the Tibetan woman to speak about the violation of human rights in Tibet. First, she only spoke in very general terms:

"I am quite young, only twenty two years old. I suffered physically under the Chinese."

I asked further if she could give concrete information on the violation of human rights. She told me her story, full of suffering:

"The Tibetans know very well about torture in Chinese prisons in Tibet. This torture is a daily practice. I was only fourteen years old when I decided to apply for a post with the military, namely in the department which deals with medical assistance. I selected this department because I expected a useful occupation and because the Chinese had promised a good salary and privileges in this sector, also for Tibetan employees.

"I was selected. When I arrived at the beginning of my training at the department, I found out that the reality did not correspond with what had been promised. Among the newly employed girls were twelve between fourteen and sixteen years, all of them very pretty. Instead of going to the hospital, we were brought to the residence of the Chinese officers. I had immediately to go to one of the officers who physically abused me.

"The Chinese officers talked all the time about rewards which we would receive later. At that time a military conference took place in Lhasa. Officers had come from Peking. Notwithstanding all our pleading, nobody listened to us. They gave us a drink of juice with which we were stunned. Afterwards I, as well as the other girls, was violated. When we woke up later and realised what had happened we felt as if we were animals. The beds were full of blood.

"For Tibetan women such a situation is terrible. There is not much other choice of escaping than committing suicide. In the room there was a fruit basket with a knife. I tried to kill myself, but I was stopped by a guard. Some of the girls who also had attempted suicide and myself were brought to the hospital. For three days I remained there and received blood transfusions."

I asked the young Tibetan woman further if it had not been possible to complain to somebody or to plead before a tribunal. She replied:

"The officers told us from the beginning that this will happen to all Tibetan girls, that nobody outside the barracks will know of it, and that nobody will believe it. It was not possible to make a complaint; we were not allowed to leave the area of the barracks. For six months we were called every evening at about seven p.m. and distributed among the officers.

"We were not allowed to talk about what happened. The majority of the Chinese officers and also the Chinese doctors took part in this abuse. The intention was to humiliate the Tibetan population.

"One of the violated girls was already four months pregnant when she was forced to have an abortion. She realised in the operating theatre that as an instrument to perform the abortion, a kind of fruit juice mixer was being used. Then the dismembered foetus was taken out piece by piece. It was already possible to recognise parts of the human body.

"Another girl tried to commit suicide by jumping out of a window. She broke a leg, which was put in plaster. When she had to be in a sick bed, and it was found out that she was also pregnant, an abortion was performed. In this hospital on some mornings more than twenty abortions were performed.

"After six months the other eleven girls and myself gathered in one room and considered what we should do. We all decided to commit suicide by drinking the white, acid liquid which is used for cleaning toilets.

Two girls, however, left the room. Security forces came, and we were put into solitary confinement and all beaten with iron rods. I still have scars from this treatment. During this time no girl received the vocational training for which she had come; training in the medical field. Later some of the girls intentionally burnt their lips with cigarettes in order to pretend to have venereal diseases and to deter Chinese officers from sexual contact. It was a terrible time. Normally it is not allowed in Tibetan society to talk about such things. But I prefer not to remain silent. The world has to know what happened, what the Chinese have done in Tibet."

Why this bestiality in the treatment of Tibetans? Why the sadism? It could be that the hatred of many Chinese officers, soldiers and officials against Tibet is profound. The discontent with their own situation, far from the Chinese homeland, often separated from their own families, may have an influence. I heard comments in Tibet that the Chinese did not have a tradition of excessive cruelty from before the time of the communist takeover of power in 1949. It has been suggested that it is not impossible that they adopted methods of sadism from the trauma of the Sino-Japanese war when such atrocities were committed by the Japanese occupying forces.

Human rights organizations, which are concerned with Tibet, accuse the Chinese especially of the following violations of human rights:

In the Tibet Autonomous Region and in other former provinces of Tibet annexed to China, thousands of Tibetan political prisoners are held without legal proceedings or after unfair legal proceedings. They are tortured, beaten, insufficiently nourished and do not receive sufficient medical treatment. Chinese officials employ the death penalty and also kill prisoners without previous court proceedings. Standard accusations of the Chinese authorities against prisoners, among them many monks and nuns, consist of the allegation that they favoured the independence of Tibet and that they had been in possession of forbidden documents, political literature and Tibetan national flags. Several prisoners have been charged with planning to translate the United Nations Universal Declaration of Human Rights into Tibetan. Some of the accused have been condemned to "change through work", others to "re-education through work", i.e. they have to do forced labour in special camps.

Those arrested and prisoners are frequently beaten and tortured in police stations, prisons and forced labour camps. They are beaten with electrically-charged batons or receive electric shocks on the soles of the feet, in the mouth or on the genitals; they are tied up for considerable periods in a single position, which cause them lingering pain. Many have been deprived of sleep and food and are forced to remain unprotected in severe cold.

Many prisoners die in prison or shortly after release. In several cases it seems to be embarrassing for the authorities when prisoners die in detention. Therefore they release persons who had been severely hurt through torture or beating, in order that they die at home.

Approximately sixty peaceful demonstrators were shot by the police between 1987 and 1989, though there had not been violent provocation. About 600 participants in demonstrations, during which violence occurred, were killed during the same period by Chinese security forces.

Legal proceedings — if there are such proceedings at

all – are normally unfair and do not correspond to minimum standards set by the human rights conventions of the United Nations.

Since 1987, everywhere in the Tibet Autonomous Region, especially in Lhasa, and also in eastern regions outside the Tibet Autonomous Region, there have been forced abortions and sterilisations of child-bearing Tibetan women. Women also are driven to accept abortions by economic sanctions. Until 1990, nomads as well as the rural population of Tibet were to a large extent exempt from the regular measures of birth control in China.

According to official statistics of 1990 in the Tibet Autonomous Region 18,000 women, that is three percent of child-bearing women, were sterilised "voluntarily". The sterilisation is carried out in many cases in hospitals immediately after a birth-giving, without the knowledge of the women concerned. The programme relates to Tibetan women who already have two children.

Tibetan women who become prégnant without official authorization have to pay bribes or will otherwise lose their jobs. Unauthorised children of such pregnancies will also be subjected to sanctions. They can be refused residence permits, which are necessary to later attend schools as well as to receive health care and food ration-cards. An abortion contravenes Buddhist values and the traditional beliefs of the Tibetans who see special merit in the birth and the upbringing of children.

There are reports of the systematic murder of children, the killing of newborn children immediately after birth. The American physician, Dr. Blake Kerr, writes that newborn infants have been killed in hospitals by alcohol injections in the soft cleft at the top of the skull.

A Tibetan doctor, Pema, reported having himself seen 400 such injections performed on Tibetan babies. Often, also, the newborn babies are suffocated or thrown into boiling water. The Tibetans call the new hospitals, which were established by the Chinese — there are all together 581 — "slaughter-houses".

After a visit by the American ambassador and members of Congress, those prisoners who had succeeded in reporting to the delegation on their commitment to the liberty of Tibet were tortured even more.

In December 1991, a Swiss Parliamentary delegation visited Drapchi Prison in Lhasa. The prisoner Tanak Jigme Sangpo, who was sixty four years old, tried to draw attention to himself by shouting "liberty for Tibet". Other prisoners joined him in these calls for freedom. Immediately, the delegation from Switzerland was asked to leave the prison. Tanak Jigme Sangpo was dragged out of his cell and brutally beaten. Other prisoners were stripped naked and kept in solitary confinement in the cold. These events had a political epilogue in the Swiss Parliament. Francois Loeb, the Chairman of the Inter-parliamentarian Group for Tibet, directed a question to the Swiss parliament because of the event. The government replied that the case was being pursued with greatest attention and that international public law forbade the punishment of a person who exercised his fundamental rights, such as freedom of speech and religious freedom.

The Austrian specialist in international public law, Professor Felix Ermacora, who had been invited by Peking to visit Tibet in early 1992 in order to write a report on the situation of human rights, had his invitation withdrawn just before his intended departure. He was finally to complete his "Mission to study the Chinese legal system, especially the situation of human rights in China/Tibet" in July 1992 jointly with the university lecturer Wolfgang Benedek. A mainly official programme had been organised, during which talks were held with the authorities and the routine touristic visits also took place. Talks with prisoners, or contacts with the population, were not possible and even not requested in order not to endanger the potential inter-locutors. The delegation was not allowed — as it had requested — to include an interpreter of Tibetan origin, but with Austrian citizenship.

Ganden Monastery before Chinese invasion

Ganden Monastery after Chinese invasion

CHINA AND THE ECOLOGY OF TIBET

"The destruction of nature and natural resources results from ignorance, greediness and a lack of respect for the living"

Dalai Lama *Universal Responsibility and the Environment*, 1989

Tibet's Traditional Respect for Nature

The territory of Tibet in its original magnitude amounts to 2,470,000 square kilometres at an average altitude of 4,000 metres above sea-level. Because of its situation in the heart of the continent of Asia, the conditions of the environment considerably influence the neighbouring countries and regions.

The Dalai Lama in several appeals has called for the conservation and protection of Tibet's natural environment. The Nobel prize committee in its decision of 1989 honoured this with the following words: "The Dalai Lama has developed his philosophy of peace from a great reverence for all things living and upon the concept of universal responsibility embracing all mankind as well as nature..."

Tibet has traditionally had a very different attitude to the environment than that of most states in the world. In 1944 Tagdra Rinpoche, the Regent of Tibet, issued the following Wildlife Conservation Decree:

"For the health of His Holiness the Dalai Lama, for the sake of the Dharma and for the benefit of all sentient beings, the village heads, officials and governors of all districts of Tibet are commanded to prevent the killing of all animals, except hyenas and wolves. The fish and otters of the water, animals of the hills and forests, the birds of the air, all animals endowed with the gift of life, whether great or small, must be protected and saved. Governors must see that the contents of this decree are carried out fully.

"Since the Iron-Dragon Year (1940), the Tibetan Government has decreed that in each and every village and town in Tibet on the eighth, fifteenth and thirtieth day of each month no domestic animals shall be killed.

In addition during the entire first and fourth months of the year people shall refrain from slaughter, as well as the fourth day of the sixth month, the twenty second day of the ninth month, and the twenty fifth day of the tenth month. On these dates no domestic animal should be slaughtered for the purposes of either selling or eating its meat. The governors and officials of each district must see to it that this injunction is faithfully observed in all regions of the Land of the Snow.

"In the past numerous decrees have been issued on this subject, however there has been no sincere attempt made by the concerned governors and district leaders to implement the contents of these decrees. As a result of the inefficiency of the governors and district officials, Nechung Chogyal (the State Oracle) stated in a trance this summer that the hunting and environmental decrees must be strictly enforced in all districts of Tibet.

"Consequently the Tibetan Government is taking more effective steps to see to it that these decrees are enforced. If the Tibetan Government hears of, or if the concerned governors report individuals who consider these decrees as routine and continue to violate them, whether that person is of high or humble status, they will be punished according to the law of the land. If the law-breakers are caught, not only they, but the governors of the district where this law is broken will be punished.

"It is possible that during winter months there will be mass slaughter of cattle. If one cannot survive without either selling or eating meat, the killing is permissible. If one can live without selling meat, the killing of yaks and other domestic animals should be avoided and district officials must make sincere attempts to look into the matter.

81

"All officials of Tibet and the public must obey and respect the ten moral and sixteen civil codes of conduct. Everyone must obey the essence of the five principles of hunting and environmental protection laws first proclaimed in the Earth-Dog Year (1896) and all the similar laws and decrees of the ancient kings of Tibet and the successive regents, supported by the Kashag, and know and carry out the responsibilities due to every individual."

The Dalai Lama explains his views on the limits of progress and consumption in a paper *Universal responsibility and the Environment*, which was published in 1989 by the University of California Press:

"It is not at all wrong for humans to use nature to make useful things, but we must not exploit nature unnecessarily. It is good to live in a house, to have medicines, and to be able to drive somewhere in a car. In the right hands, a machine is not a luxury, but something very useful. A camera, for example, can be used to make pictures that promote understanding. But everything has its limit. Too much consumption or effort to make money is not good. Neither is too much contentment. In principle, contentment is a goal, but pure contentment becomes almost like suicide, doesn't it? I think the Tibetans had, in certain fields, too much contentment. And we lost our country. These days we cannot afford too much contentment about the environment.

"Peace and survival of life on earth as we know it are threatened by human activities that lack a commitment to humanitarian values. Destruction of nature and natural resources results from ignorance, greed, and lack of respect for the earth's living things."

The British envoy to Tibet in the 1940s, Hugh

Richardson, wrote that the Tibetan system produced a people the majority of whom made efforts to live as much as possible in harmony with nature, not against it.

Especially from the many NGOs, which have been established to help Tibet, a strong interest in the protection of Tibet's vulnerable eco-system exists. Except from the tropical rain-forest in Brazil, there is probably no region in the world on which the interest of ecologists is so much focused as on the Tibetan high plateau.

Over-Exploitation and Loss of Ecological Equilibrium

The main problem seems to be the massive deforestation: The forest land of Tibet has been diminished since 1949 from 221,800 square kilometers by about fifty percent to 134,000 in 1985. Deforestation takes place mainly in the eastern mountains of the Tibetan high plateau. Until very recently, this region was almost exclusively inhabited by Tibetans. In the meantime many Chinese live there, who came from the provinces of Sichuan, Gansu and Yunnan.

In the north, in the Tibetan Amdo province, in 1949 3,971,500 hectares of forest still existed. In the area of Ngapa alone from 1955 until the middle of the eighties, forests of 2.2 million hectares, i.e. 340 million cubic metres, have been reduced to 1.17 million hectares, i.e. 180 million cubic metres.

The radical deforestation has caused strong erosion, which in the meantime harms the agricultural use of the soil. Many landslides have occurred. Rivers changed their course and took with them fertile earth. The waters of the Brahmaputra, Salween, Mekong, Yellow

River and Yangtse now run with greater speed downstream. This has already caused devastating inundations in the lowlands of China, India and Bangladesh. The deforestation by the Chinese in Eastern Tibet is believed to be the cause of the severe inundations in Bangladesh. In early summer of 1992 heavy inundations occurred also in China. Already, in 1991, more than 3,000 Chinese are believed to have lost their lives in the floods and millions to have lost their homes. The radical deforestation of Eastern Tibet can at least partly be considered as the cause of this catastrophe. The Yellow River and the Yangtse, which run through large parts of China, have their origins in Tibet. In the longterm, the deforestation of Tibet threatens to contribute to a change in the climate.

Another serious threat to the sensitive ecological equilibrium of Tibet is the massive population transfer of Chinese, especially into Eastern Tibet. Many Tibetan farmers and nomads have been driven out by the newly-settled Chinese and forced to find new pastures at higher locations. Because of the collectivization of agriculture after the takeover by the Chinese, Tibetans have also been forced to allow a larger number of animals to graze on a smaller pasturage.

Building and extension of roads after the introduction of a market economy enhanced the conditions for marketing meat, and the gains increased. This, however, resulted in overgrazing, which in the medium-term will have negative repercussions. The quality of the pastures has already deteriorated because of the intensive use, and − according to the findings of Chinese scientists − already a pasturage of double the size of ten years ago is today necessary to feed the same number of animals. As a further consequence of this overgrazing, the topsoil has become so thin that the wind has carried away the humus and the desertification of large areas has occurred.

Because the Chinese settlers have hunted intensively, and some Tibetans did not respect the Buddhist precept not to kill and also hunted, many large mammals have become extinct in the meantime. Therefore small rodents have rapidly reproduced. They have fed on the grass roots below the surface, so extensive areas of grass have died and the desertification has rapidly spread.

Disdain for Nature and Religion

Before the Chinese invasion there was a tabu in Tibet in respect of excessive violations against nature and the environment. This was a direct consequence of the Buddhist knowledge of the mutual dependency of all human, animal and plant life as well as of the non-sentient elements of nature, i.e. mountains, rivers, lakes, air and the radiant sun.

This tabu proved so strong that for centuries Tibetans did not exploit their mineral resources. They were convinced that such exploitation would infuriate the deities, cause consequently damage to humans, and deprive the land itself of its natural vigour.

The Chinese have nevertheless promoted mining, from which they benefited to a large extent.

During the Cultural Revolution the Chinese forced many monks, nuns and lay Tibetans, to violate the commandment not to slaughter any living beings by ordering them to kill small animals and insects on their way to work and in the fields. They had to fulfill a special quota, and to daily report the number of animals they had killed. This included the obligation to produce the legs or wings of the animals. If the quota was not fulfilled they were severely punished.

During the 1970s the ecological consequences of the senseless killing of birds became evident: The numbers of insects increased massively, because they had no natural enemies. Swarms of insects destroyed the harvests.

Lama Anagarika Govinda aptly summarised the dilemma of the ecological destruction of Tibet:

"Tibet chose her own way; namely to renounce the conquest of the owners of nature... Instead she decided to cultivate and develop that interior knowledge which is the true source of all human culture, knowledge and achievements... This is the way in which Tibetans view the problems of the future of humanity, problems which now confront us on a global scale."

In his Five-Point Peace Plan for Tibet, which he announced in 1987, the Dalai Lama asked for the protection of Tibet's natural environment and the renunciation by China of use of Tibet for the production of nuclear weapons and the dumping of nuclear waste:

"The Tibetans have a great respect for all forms of life. This inherent feeling is enhanced by the Buddhist faith, which prohibits the harming of all sentient beings, whether human or animal. Prior to the Chinese invasion, Tibet was an unspoiled wilderness sanctuary in a unique natural environment. Sadly, in the past decades the wildlife and the forests of Tibet have been almost totally destroyed by the Chinese. The effects on Tibet's delicate environment have been devastating. What little is left in Tibet must be protected and efforts must be made to restore the environment to its balanced state.

"China uses Tibet for the production of nuclear weapons and may also have started dumping nuclear waste in Tibet. China plans to dispose not only of its own nuclear waste but also that of other countries, which have already agreed to pay Peking to dispose of their toxic materials.

"The dangers this presents are obvious. Not only living generations, but future generations are threatened by China's lack of concern for Tibet's unique and delicate environment."

The Chinese Government has again taken up the construction of a hydro-electric power station at the Yamdrok Tso Lake. From the lake a six kilometer long tunnel has to be built through a mountain, through which the water will descend for 846 metres to the Yarlung-Tsangpo River. There are plans for an initial 15,000 kilowatt generator and then by the year 2,000, six generators of altogether 90,000 kilowatts. At times of the day when the need for energy is not very great, the water is supposed to be pumped back into the lake. The Tibetans fear an appalling dirtying of the turquoise-blue waters of the holy lake through the muddy brown inflow of recycled water.

It has been calculated that — if the turbines once function — the water-level of the lake which is 800 square kilometers in size, will sink annually by 7.6 centimetres. The project, which began in 1985, had been stopped after the intervention of the Panchen Lama in 1986. The Panchen Lama had insisted that the construction of the hydro-electric power station would be very costly and be of no benefit to Tibetans and, moreover, damage the environment severely. In August 1989, only a few months after the death of the Panchen Lama, the project was again taken up. China requested Norway and Switzerland to finance the project, which is estimated to cost U.S. $ 140 million.

Yamdrok Tso is one of the holiest lakes in Tibet and a place of veneration for generations of pilgrims. The electricity which is generated here will mainly be beneficial to the Chinese in Lhasa and the surrounding areas, because it is principally their apartments that are connected to the power supply system. The Tibetans themselves use mainly yak dung or wood as energy sources. Because of the long spells of sunshine solar energy also has a great potential.

The Chinese have difficulties in reacting reasonably concerning the accusations arising from the destruction of the environment and the over-exploitation of natural resources, especially deforestation. Peking wants to show co-operation in certain fields, and therefore recently declared a huge territory in the North of Lhasa as a nature reserve.

TIBET AND THE WEST

"Smaller states sometimes have the bigger heart"
Dalai Lama in a conversation with the author, 1990

The Tibet Myth

In 1811, the Russian Imperial Court Counsellor and Professor of Geography and Statistics in Weimar, Adam Christian Gaspari, wrote in his book on geography about the Tibetans:

"The Tibetans are not without knowledge, have high schools, which are also visited by foreigners from China, from Koschotei and from Kashmir. Magic is the science which they esteem more than anything else."

For centuries Tibet has instilled a special fascination in the West, as well as in peoples of other parts of the world. Tibet was even a symbol of mystical knowledge about the meaning and goal of our existence.

In the extraordinary temples of Angkor in Cambodia, of Borobudur in Java, to mention only two examples, and everywhere in Asia the heavily symbolic model of Mount Kailash, the stylised replica of the holy mountain Meru, can be found.

In the great Hindu epos Mahabharata, Mount Kailash is thus described: "He shines like the morning sun and like fire without smoke, unmeasurable and unattainable by men, who are to be encumbered with sins." On his summit stands Warga, the heavenly city of Indra, the old Vedic god of rain and storm. Here lived the gods and heavenly spirits under the leadership of Brahma. Staircases of stars led up to the mountain Meru. In the lower spheres the souls of the deceased waited for reincarnation.

The holy mountain Kailash also has central significance for the religion of the Jains and for the Shaman Bön religion of Tibet. News of Mount Kailash first came to the West only in the seventeenth century. Each generation has created its own, imaginary image of Tibet:

The inaccessible forbidden land which, unlike many other countries in Asia, was not a European colony. For a long time it was only possible to reach Tibet after enormous difficulties and trials. Only few adventurers or great explorers succeeded in reaching Lhasa. Even the Swedish explorer Sven Hedin, who for many years tried with various expeditions to reach Lhasa, remained unsuccessful.

Legends were created concerning the mysterious country. A novel by James Hilton, *Lost Horizon*, on the mystical valley of Shangri-la, which was supposed to be located in Tibet, fascinated its readers. In the West there was a desire for an unattainable country, for a Garden of Eden of which one could dream. According to Tibetan tradition there is a mystical country beyond Tibet with the name of Shambala which, however, is far from any reality.

The German god of thunder, Thor, corresponds more or less to Indra, the Vedic god, who – as mentioned above – is supposed to be enthroned on the holy mountain Kailash.

The National-Socialists in Germany imitated a Buddhist and Hindu symbol, the swastika, by reversing it and making it their symbol. In reality the swastika symbolizes the course of the four holy rivers of Asia, the Brahmaputra, the Ganges, the Indus and the Sutlej, the source of which flows from Mount Kailash to Lake Manasarovar, before spreading and flowing in the direction of the four points of the compass. Furthermore the swastika is supposed to be clearly visible on the south flank of Mount Kailash. The swastika is depicted in many Tibetan temples – for example on a mosaic of semi-precious stones in Tashilhunpo, the famous monastery of the Panchen Lama in Shigatse.

In Dharamsala, the proper meaning from the view-point of faithful Tibetans was explained to me. The swastika serves as a symbolic instrument to open and to turn over the book of the Dharma, the teachings of Buddha, i.e. to progress on the path to enlightenment. A reversed swastika, that is to say a National-Socialist swastika, ought to have the opposite effect; i.e. the closing of the dharma, the teaching of Buddha. This could cause nothing else than the greatest disaster.

In the 1960s, the hippies who had arrived in the foothills of the Himalayas, in Nepal and India, became enthusiastic about what they understood as the spiritual message of Tibet. The wording of a song of the Beatles was taken from the *Book of the Dead of the Tibetans* – the *Bardo Thödol*.

The mystification of Tibet could partly be based on respect for the strength of faith and the dimension of spirituality on the roof of the world.

The well-known French researcher on Tibetan questions, Alexandra David-Neel, who travelled as a Buddhist nun for years through Tibet, and Lama Anagarika Govinda write in their books about mysterious practices and magic in Tibet. This especially concerns the ability to levitate by meditative force, and the practice of *Tum-mo* yoga, a tantric discipline, by which heat is created, and finally the so-called *Lung-gom-pa* runners – men running very fast in a state of elevation during trance – which is practiced especially in the monastery of Shalu in Southern Central Tibet. Such lamas, trained in *Lung-gom-pa*, who were carriers of secret information, are supposed to have covered hundreds of kilometers every day. When, in 1992, I visited the monastery of Shalu, which now can be comfortably reached by jeep, there was nothing to remind anymore of this mysterious tradition.

The Dalai Lama in his autobiography gives an overview of such magic and mysterious phenomena, such as the practice of *Tum-mo* yoga.

He had permitted the director of the department of behavioral medicine of the Harvard Medical School, Dr. Herbert Benson, to investigate those practices scientifically by observing Tibetan lamas who live in hermitages in Dharamsala, Ladakh and Sikkim. The technique of yoga consists in developing the aptitude to turn off several levels of consciousness and to concentrate on a few, more subtle levels of consciousness. One of the essential objectives of tantric practices consists in allowing the performer to "experience" death. It is believed that in this way the strongest spiritual experiences can be gained.

Dr. Benson measured the increase in body temperature of the lamas who practiced *Tum-mo* yoga and discovered that the escalation measured ten degrees centigrade. So they were able to sit nude in the snow and to dry a wet sheet with their body heat. Alexandra David-Neel and the French explorer of Tibet, Amaury de Riencourt, report that this drying of sheets by the temperature of the body was developed by lamas — sitting nude in the snow — into a kind of competition. Some lamas could dry a dozen or more sheets in a nightly session. The scientific explanation by Dr. Benson for these events is that, apparently, the practitioner of *Tum-mo* yoga is able to burn off "brown fat" in his body and hence generate heat. This is a phenomenon which, it was believed, only animals which hibernate — especially bears — were able to produce.

As I was told in several conversations, many of the intellectuals in Tibet also believe in this practice, whereas stories of "fast runners" are dismissed as legends.

The belief of Tibetans in oracles is deeply-rooted. The tradition, which was mainly cultivated in the Nechung monastery in Lhasa, is based on Shamanist origins. Dorje Drakden, one of the protector deities of the Dalai Lama, is believed to reveal himself through the Nechung Oracle.

The Dalai Lama in his autobiography explains the "magic and mysterious" aspects of Tibetan Buddhism in the following way: If scientific methods were not able to detect his thoughts, this did not mean that he had no thoughts and that it was not possible to discover something about them with another method. Through spiritual training the Tibetans had gained special experience in this respect and developed techniques, to cause events to happen, which science could not yet explain suitably.

What can the West learn from Tibet?

I was interested in the question, of what the West could learn from Tibet, especially concerning so-called basic values in politics and their ethical basis in religion. I asked the Dalai Lama if the West could learn from the experience and wisdom as well as from the marked influence of Buddhism in politics in Asia.

The Dalai Lama replied: "In looking at the experience in Buddhist countries, for example in Thailand, I am sceptical and I am even more sceptical when we consider Cambodia or Laos and also Viet Nam, where some years ago as consequence of politics the suffering among the people became so great. We cannot claim that traditionally Buddhist countries provide especially good conditions to enhance the well-being of their population by good government."

As to my question concerning the position of the Buddhist teaching as related to Marxism, the Dalai Lama replied:

"I believe that our Buddhism, which does not know any veneration of God, but is in its nature atheist, and the main content of which is ethical knowledge, how man should live, is predestined to challenge Marxism, for which man does not count, but for which abstract ideology has become an end in itself. Finally Buddhism will prove to be superior to Marxism, because for Buddhism the most important matters will always be man and the care for the individual."

We talked for a while about the question of the ethical basis of politics. The Dalai Lama commented:

"I discussed this question some time ago with Indian politicians who are not religiously engaged. They claimed that, if for example two or three religious fanatics withdraw somewhere into solitude, perhaps even as hermits, to reflect on the role of religion in the world — and you know," the Dalai Lama smiled, "by doing so, of course it can happen, that somebody becomes crazy — this incident would remain completely irrelevant for the politics of their countries. But what, I asked, if two or three politicians, who are responsible for the fate of their countries and do not withdraw from the world, suddenly become crazy?" The Dalai Lama laughed his strong, hearty laugh and exclaimed with determination: "An ethical basis for politics is necessary."

The words of the Dalai Lama in his small booklet *Compassion and the Individual*, which appeared in

1991, appear especially meaningful. In only a few pages he describes how each man confronted with spiritual and physical suffering can achieve a state of happiness. The Dalai Lama recommends in this respect the maximum of selfless compassion. This fully corresponds to his role in Tibetan Buddhism as an emanation of Avalokiteshvara, Bodhisattva of compassion.

The Dalai Lama writes:

"Though sometimes people laugh when I say it, I myself always want more friends. I love smiles. Because of this I have the problem of knowing how to make more friends and how to get more smiles, in particular, genuine smiles. For there are many kinds of smile, such as sarcastic, artificial or diplomatic smiles. Many smiles produce no feeling of satisfaction, and sometimes they can even create suspicion or fear, can't they? But a genuine smile really gives us a feeling of freshness and is, I believe, unique to human beings. If these are the smiles we want, then we ourselves must create the reasons for them to appear."

The Dalai Lama then pleads for individual happiness, which could contribute in a deep and effective way to the general improvement of human society:

"Because we all share an identical need for love, it is possible to feel that anybody we meet, in whatever circumstances, is a brother or sister. No matter how new the face or how different the dress and behaviour, there is no significant division between us and other people. It is foolish to dwell on external differences, because our basic natures are the same... I believe that at every level of society — familial, tribal, national and international — the key to a happier and more successful world is the growth of compassion. We do not need to become more religious, nor do we need to believe in ideology. All that is necessary is for each of us to develop our good human qualities.

"I try to treat whoever I meet as an old friend. This gives me a genuine feeling of happiness. It is the practice of compassion."

The traditional thought patterns and ideologies in the West — shaped by capitalism or the market economy — as well as, until recently, those of the Soviet Union and its satellite states, determined by Marxism-Leninism, see or saw the essential goal of private and collective efforts in permanent material improvements. The new ecological movements see their objective in halting the irretrievable destruction of nature, and hence of the fundamentals of life for humanity though reckless and uncontrolled economic growth.

It is not impossible that the way proposed by the Dalai Lama, i.e. of growth, of an increase in compassion — as key to a happier and more successful future — will gain special significance worldwide. This way of increasing compassion does not, however, claim to be a purified substitute ideology — representing, as a result of a synthesis of the two antagonistic ideologies, the capitalist and the Marxist-Leninist — with the help of which it would be possible to master the problems of the future. This would not correspond to the modesty or to the realism of the Dalai Lama.

The way is founded on the teachings developed by Buddha 2,500 years ago about our relations with our fellow men, all sentient beings, nature and the environment. Even if the Dalai Lama always emphasizes that he is only a simple, humble monk, the way of compassion indicated by him could help to find a useful ethical starting point for a solution, which could become the common denominator, encompassing individual solutions for many of the great problems of our time and of the time to come, especially in respect to ecological questions.

The West can certainly learn in this respect from Tibetan Buddhism.

Worldwide Support from NGOs

In 1990, in Dharamsala a conference of NGOs from many countries took place. Surpassing all expectations, more than forty organisations attended the conference. Particularly prominent among the participants were A.P. Venkateswaran, the former Foreign Secretary of India and ambassador in Peking, as well as Petra Kelly and Gert Bastian from the Green Party in Germany.

The work focused on the preparation of a strategy for the nineties. The main purpose of this strategy is the worldwide co-ordination of efforts of the Tibetans as well as the friends of Tibet.

It was decided that as many states as possible should be encouraged to invite the Dalai Lama for official visits; that a computerised information service for Tibet should be established; that the world public should be informed about the threatening destruction of Tibet's environment; that co-ordination among the Chinese dissidents living in the West should be strengthened; and, that the influence of the United Nations and other governmental organizations as well as NGOs should be strengthened. The first priority should be protests against the violation of human rights and the enforcement of the right of self-determination for the Tibetan people.

Draft resolutions were circulated with a recommendation for their worldwide adoption by national parliaments.

Since 1989 many of these NGO's have worked with great engagement for an improvement of the fate of the Tibetans in Tibet as well as for the protection of the environment and the end of the ecological destruction in Tibet. International NGOs contributed to a considerable extent to the documentation of human rights violations. A report submitted for the session of the Commission on Human Rights by ECOSOC (Economic and Social Council of the United Nations) in January 1992, reprinted contributions of seven organisations which enjoy consultative status at ECOSOC, namely,

— Amnesty International;
— The Association of Disabled Peoples International, Human Rights Advocates, International Federation of Human Rights, International Federation of Women Lawyers, Pax Christi International Education Development, Inc. and Liberation;
— Habitat International Coalition;
— International Fellowship of Reconciliation;
— International League for Human Rights;
— Law Association for Asia and the Western Pacific (LAWASIA);
— Minority Rights Group

These contributions replied to a document by the representative of the Ministry of Foreign Affairs of the People's Republic of China of August 1991 concerning the situation of human rights in Tibet, which can hardly be surpassed in its simplistic presentation and endless repetition of stories about Tibet's feudal past. The relevant questions are simply omitted. Concerning the question of Tibet, China is on the defensive.

In May 1995, the World Parliamentarian Conference on Tibet (WPCT) held its second World Convention in the Lithuanian capital, Vilnius: eighty members from twenty one parliaments all over the world were represented. The Chairman of the Assembly of the Tibetan People's Deputies, Professor Samdhong Rinpoche, presented the keynote address, confiding that the situation in Tibet had become so desperate that a wholesome return of Tibetans to Tibet, including their leaders, was now being contemplated in order to carry out further non-violent protest including a campaign of civil disobedience. The sole objective of this campaign was meant to be the persuasion of the Chinese authorities to enter into meaningful dialogue without preconditions, to achieve self-determination for Tibetans.

The medium of film, especially a film which is of a high standard from the artistic point of view, can make an important contribution to support Tibet by explaining the situation in Tibet to a huge number of spectators. In this respect the movies produced by Franz-Christoph Gierke, whom I met in Dharamsala while waiting for an audience with the Dalai Lama, are significant. F.-C. Gierke has made beautiful films about Tibet, through which the spectator can become aware of the spirituality and the mystical aspects of Tibetan Buddhism.

Lord of the Dance, Destroyer of Illusions is a film about the tantric rituals in Thupten Chöling monastery, which is situated south of Mount Everest in Nepal. Previously the monastery was to the north of Mount Everest in Tibet and was called Rongbo. In 1959, the abbot Trulshig Rinpoche escaped with hundreds of monks and an invaluable inventory of religious artifacts to Nepal and rebuilt the monastery. Hence the unique tradition of the monastery and its special knowledge of tantric practice were preserved.

Another film *Les Cavaliers du Vent*, is a documentary about Tibetan provinces outside the Tibet Autonomous Region, which have been formally annexed by China. The French actress Isabelle Adjani voices the very lyrical text. She quotes poems by the Indian mystic and great teacher Padmasambhava, who lived in Tibet in the eighth century A.D. F.C. Gierke explained me that he was able to film these sequences when he was in Tibet to make a movie about Alexandra David-Neel, the French explorer of Tibet. The Chinese supervisors had not realised his intent. The film is an impressive document. In Paris, for many weeks, people had to queue in front of cinemas to get tickets as it was always sold out.

Because of the better information on Tibet, there is more and more interest in the West about Tibet and its unique, threatened civilisation, and there is also an increasing engagement for its people.

American Congress, the United Nations Commission on Human Rights, European Parliament

The American Senate and the House of Representatives on 23 May 1991 passed the following resolution:

"Whereas Tibet has maintained throughout its history a distinctive national, cultural, and religious identity, separate from that of China;

Whereas Chinese archival documents and traditional dynastic histories, including those pertaining to periods of Manchu and Mongol rule, never refer to Tibet as being made 'an integral part' of China;

Whereas several countries, including Mongolia, Bhutan, Nepal, British India, and Czarist Russia recognised Tibet as an independent nation or dealt with Tibet independently of any Chinese government;

Whereas in 1949-50, China launched an armed invasion of Tibet in contravention of international law;

Whereas at the time of the Chinese occupation, Tibet possessed all the attributes of statehood under international law, including a defined territory, population, independent government, and the ability to conduct domestic affairs and independent international relations, as found in 1960 by the International Commission of Jurists;

Whereas in 1959, members of the Tibetan Government, including the head of state, the Dalai Lama, sought political asylum in India following a national uprising against the Chinese occupying forces, and established a government in exile which continues to operate today and is recognised by the Tibetan people as the only legitimate Government of Tibet;

Whereas it is the policy of the United States to oppose aggression and other illegal uses of force by one country against the sovereignty of another, and to condemn violations of international law, including the illegal occupation of one country by another;

Whereas in the 1950s and 1960s the United States repeatedly condemned what it characterised as China's aggression against Tibet and actively supported the United Nations in both condemning China and calling for Tibet's right to self-determination in General Assembly resolutions 1353 (1959), 1723 (1961), and 2079 (1965);

Whereas on December 16, 1961, at the United Nations, United States Ambassador Plimpton summarised the official United States position on Tibet, stating, The United States believes that our objectives must include the restoration of human rights of the Tibetan people and their natural right of self-determination;

Whereas China's illegal occupation of Tibet continues to this day;

Now, therefore, be it

Resolved by the House of Representatives (the Senate concurring) That it is the sense of Congress that Tibet, including those areas incorporated into the Chinese provinces of Sichuan, Yunnan, Gansu, and Qinghai, is an occupied country under established principles of international law whose true representatives are the Dalai Lama and the Tibetan Government-in-Exile as recognised by the Tibetan people."

In October 1991 President Bush signed a "US State Department Authorisation Act", which refers to the above resolution.

This resolution is of special interest because it mentions also the Tibetan territories which were incorporated into the Chinese provinces Sichuan, Yunnan, Gansu and Qinghai, regions, which — according to Peking's will — are not part of the "Tibet Autonomous Region". The annexation of these Tibetan territories was partly carried out by force even before the foundation of the People's Republic of China in 1949. Tibet was divided into six administrative districts under the Communist rule of China:

Tibet Autonomous Region
In 1950 forces of the Chinese People's Liberation Army conquered the central province U-Tsang. In 1965 the Chinese proclaimed the province as "Tibet Autonomous Region".

Qinghai Chinese Province

Even before 1949 the Kuomintang of General Chiang Kai-shek claimed the largest part of the Amdo Tibetan province.

Kanhlo Tibetan Autonomous Prefecture

The prefecture Kanhlo was part of the Amdo Tibetan region. It was incorporated again as an autonomous Tibetan prefecture into the Chinese province Gansu.

Ngapa Tibetan Autonomous Prefecture

Ngapa was part of the Amdo Tibetan region. Even before 1950 Ngapa was incorporated as an autonomous Tibetan prefecture into the Sichuan Chinese Province.

Kanzi Tibetan Autonomous Prefecture

Kanzi was part of the Kham Tibetan region. The People's Liberation Army conquered Kanzi even before the seizure of power in Peking in 1949. Kanzi was incorporated in the years 1950-54 into the Chinese province Sinkiang, and later, from 1954-57 separated again to become an "autonomous Tibetan prefecture" part of the Chinese province of Sichuan.

Dechen Tibetan Autonomous Prefecture

Dechen was part of the Kham Tibetan region. In 1949 it was occupied by forces of the Chinese liberation army and incorporated as a Tibetan autonomous prefecture into the Chinese province of Yunnan. Much fighting occurred here even before 1950.

On the territory of the original state of Tibet, such as it existed before the partition, there live today around six million Tibetans and eight million Chinese. In the previous territories of Amdo province, which have now been given to Qinghai and Gansu, there live today 800,000 Tibetans and 2.5 million Chinese. In the former province of Kham, there are 3.3 million Tibetans as compared to three million Chinese. In all major cities there are already more Chinese than Tibetans. According to Chinese estimates more than fifty eight percent of the inhabitants of Lhasa are Chinese. In the city of Chamdo, capital of Kham, there are even said to be ninety five percent of Chinese. The Tibetans have become a minority in their own country.

In February 1992 President Bush met the Chinese Prime Minister Li Peng. One of the results of the meeting was that the United States suddenly changed its attitude at the Human Rights Commission of the United Nations in Geneva: The American ambassador opposed the endeavours of the twelve European Community-states, eight other European states and three Central American states, to pass a resolution in which China is explicitly criticised because of the violation of human rights in Tibet. The ambassador argued that while the USA was committed to the respect of human rights in Tibet, this commitment, however, was not limited to Tibet but encompassed all China.

The American Ambassador to the United Nations in Geneva, J. Kenneth Blackwell, said in an interview with *The South China Morning Post* that from a moral point of view it could not be justified to single out Tibetans if millions of Chinese also suffered. At the same time America criticised the restriction of freedom of speech for dissidents in China.

Instead of proposing a new resolution, in which China would be criticised because of the violation of human rights in Tibet as well as in China itself, the representative of the United States at the United Nations in Geneva simply did nothing. Members of the American delegation in Geneva intimated, however, that the instructions to act in favour of Peking came directly from President Bush. It is possible that President Bush expected concessions in return from Li Peng, especially a possible signature of the Nuclear Non-proliferation Treaty by China, as well as concessions concerning trade questions.

Pakistan, which enjoys very good relations with China, introduced a procedural request in the Human Rights Commission of the United Nations, asking that the Commission should not take up the proposed resolution. It claimed that the resolution, which was introduced by the European Community, was an attempt to assert the independence of Tibet, and that therefore it was not a question of human rights.

The text of the resolution read as follows: "The Commission on Human Rights,

Guided by the principles of the Charter of the United Nations, the Universal Declaration of Human Rights and other United Nations conventions, declarations and resolutions on human rights, recalling Sub-Commission resolution 1991/10 of 23 August 1991 and other relevant United Nations resolutions, concerned at continuing reports of violations of human rights and fundamental freedoms in Tibet which threaten the distinct cultural, religious and ethnic identity of the Tibetans,

1. Takes note of the summary records of the debates on this question during the forty-third session of the Sub-Commission;

2. Also takes note of the Secretary-General's note (E/CN.4/1992/37) on the subject;

3. Further takes note of the reports of the Special Rapporteur on torture (E/CN.4/1992/17), on summary or arbitrary executions (E./CN.4/1992/30), on religious intolerance (E/CN.4/1992/52) and the report of the Working Group on Enforced or Involuntary Disappearances (E/CN.4/1992/18);

4. Calls on the Government of the People's Republic of China to take measures to ensure the full observance of human rights and fundamental freedoms of the Tibetans;
5. Invites the Government of the People's Republic of China to continue to respond to requests by special rapporteurs for information;
6. Requests the Secretary-General to submit a report to the Commission on Human Rights at its forty-ninth session on the situation in Tibet."

Of the fifty three states entitled to vote in the UN Commission, twenty seven voted in favour of the request of Pakistan; fifteen states, all of them Western, as well as Japan and Costa Rica, voted against and ten states abstained. Therefore the resolution could not be considered.

On the day when the result became known Richard Schifter (the highest official in the American State Department in charge of human rights questions) resigned.

As a result of the procedural request of Pakistan, which was adopted, the Commission on Human Rights of the United Nations could not adopt a resolution in which China was criticised. However, China must have noted, finally, that the world today – rather than turning away indifferently – is very conscious of what is happening in Tibet.

In 1993 and 1994 again the EC and other states sponsored resolutions on the situation of human rights at the Commission for Human Rights of United Nations in Geneva. They were, however, defeated again on procedural grounds by a "no action motion" introduced by China and its prominent allies, among which Pakistan played an important role.

In March 1995, a resolution concerning the situation of human rights in China in general with special reference to the situation of the Tibetan people was introduced again by the European Union (the organization which emerged from the EC, now comprising fifteen states). For the first time, China's "no action motion" was defeated with twenty two votes in favour of China's motion, twenty two against, and nine abstentions. Russia first supported the resolution by voting against the Chinese demand. However, when the vote on the adoption of the resolution finally took place, Russia had changed course. This meant twenty one votes against the resolution, twenty votes in favour and twelve abstentions.

Though the resolution failed to be adopted by one vote, the situation for China has become precarious.

Since 1987 the European Parliament has adopted nine resolutions on Tibet.

The first resolution reflects the constructive attitude of the European Parliament towards China, by proposing a balanced and fair settlement of the question of Tibet on the basis of the Dalai Lama's five point programme:

The European Parliament

1) Gravely concerned by the recent disturbances in Lhasa which are reported to have caused many deaths,

2) Recalling that both during the early days of the Chinese occupation in the 1950s and during the Cultural Revolution the Tibetan religion and culture were brutally repressed,

3) Noting the policy of tolerance which has been shown in recent times by the Chinese authorities towards the Tibetan Buddhist religion by the reconstruction

of certain monasteries, as well as the growing participation of Tibetans in the administration of the Autonomous Region,

4) Having regard to the new legal provisions of 1984 concerning the status of autonomous regions in China,

5) Calling attention to the Dalai Lama's five-point programme on the status of Tibet and relations between the Chinese and Tibetan people,

    a) Urges the Chinese Government to respect the rights of the Tibetans to religious freedom and cultural autonomy,

    b) Considers that the Dalai Lama's five-point programme could well form the basis of a settlement,

    c) Instructs its President to forward this resolution to the Commission, the Council and the Government of the People's Republic of China.

The 1995 resolution in particular demanded China to meet the demands of the Tibetan people in respect to the Chinese settlement policy in Tibet, to the protection of human rights, to the preservation of Tibetan culture, and to the right of selfdetermination of Tibetans in accordance with the UN Charter and the UN Pact for Civil and Political Rights.

Nobel Prize for Peace

In the autumn of 1989 the Dalai Lama received the Nobel Prize for Peace. China had threatened Norway that if the King of Norway were to hand over this prize to the Dalai Lama there would be serious consequences for their bilateral relations. Norway, however, was not swayed.

The key sentence of the reasons why the Nobel Committee granted the Nobel Peace Prize to the Dalai Lama was:

"The Dalai Lama has developed his philosophy of peace from a great reverence for all things living and upon the concept of universal responsibility embracing all mankind as well as nature..."

In December 1989 the Dalai Lama delivered the following speech in Oslo in which it can be clearly felt that the God-king of Tibet is guided, in respect of his political thinking, by his position as the reincarnation of Avalokiteshvara, Bodhisattva of Compassion:

"Your Majesty, Members of the Nobel Committee, Brothers and Sisters,

I am very happy to be here with you today and receive the Nobel Prize for Peace. I feel honoured, humbled and deeply moved that you should give this important prize to a simple monk from Tibet. I am no one special. But I believe the prize is a recognition of the true value of altruism, love and compassion and non-violence which I try to practice, in accordance with the teachings of the Buddha and the great sages of India and Tibet.

"I accept the prize with profound gratitude on behalf of the oppressed everywhere and for all those who struggle for freedom and work for world peace. I accept it as a tribute to the man who founded the modern tradition of non-violent action for change – Mahatma Gandhi – whose life taught and inspired me. And, of course, I accept it on behalf of the six million Tibetan people, my brave countrymen and women inside Tibet, who have suffered and continue to suffer so much. They confront a calculated and systematic strategy aimed at the destruction of their national and cultural identities. The prize reaffirms our conviction that with truth, courage and determination as our weapons, Tibet will be liberated.

"No matter what part of the world we come from, we are all basically the same human beings. We all seek happiness and try to avoid suffering. We have the same basic human needs and concerns. All of us human beings want freedom and the right to determine our own destiny as individuals and as peoples. That is human nature. The great changes that are taking place everywhere in the world, from Eastern Europe to Africa, are a clear indication of this.

"In China the popular movement for democracy was crushed by brutal force in June this year. But I do not believe the demonstrations were in vain, because the spirit of freedom was rekindled among the Chinese people and China cannot escape the impact of this spirit of freedom sweeping many parts of the world. The brave students and their supporters showed the Chinese leadership and the world the human face of that great nation.

"Last week a number of Tibetans were once again sentenced to prison terms up to nineteen years at a mass show trial, possibly intended to frighten the population before today's event. Their only 'crime' was the expression of the widespread desire of Tibetans for the restoration of their beloved country's independence.

"The suffering of our people during the past forty years of occupation is well documented. Ours has been a long struggle. We know our cause is just. Because violence can only breed more violence and suffering, our struggle must remain non-violent and free of hatred. We are trying to end the suffering of our people, not to inflict suffering upon others.

"It is with this in mind that I proposed negotiations between Tibet and China on numerous occasions. In 1987, I made specific proposals in a Five-Point Plan for the restoration of peace and human rights in Tibet. This included the conversion of the entire Tibetan plateau into a Zone of Ahimsa, a sanctuary of peace and non-violence where human beings and nature can live in peace and harmony.

"Last year, I elaborated on that plan in Strasbourg, at the European Parliament. I believe the ideas I expressed on those occasions are both realistic and reasonable, although they have been criticised by some of my people as being too conciliatory. Unfortunately, China's leaders have not responded positively to the suggestions we have made, which included important concessions. If this continues we will be compelled to reconsider our position.

"Any relationship between Tibet and China will have to be based on the principle of equality, respect, trust and mutual benefit. It will also have to be based on the principle which the wise rulers of Tibet and China laid down in a treaty as early as 823 AD carved on the pillar which still stands today in front of the Jokhang, Tibet's holiest shrine, in Lhasa, that 'Tibetans will live happily in the great land of Tibet, and the Chinese will live happily in the great land of China'.

"As a Buddhist monk, my concern extends to all members of the human family and, indeed, to all sentient beings who suffer. I believe all suffering is caused by ignorance. People inflict pain on others in the selfish pursuit of their happiness or satisfaction. Yet true happiness comes from a sense of inner peace and contentment, which in turn must be achieved through the cultivation of altruism, of love and compassion and elimination of ignorance, selfishness and greed.

"The problems we face today, violent conflicts, destruction of nature, poverty, hunger, and so on, are human created problems which can be resolved through human effort, understanding and the development of a sense of brotherhood and sisterhood. We need to cultivate a universal responsibility for one another and the planet we share. Although I have found my own Buddhist religion helpful in generating love and compassion, even for those we consider our enemies, I am convinced that everyone can develop a good heart and a sense of universal responsibility with or without religion.

"With the ever-growing impact of science on our lives, religion and spirituality have a greater role to play, reminding us of our humanity. There is no contradiction between the two. Each gives us valuable insights into the other. Both science and teachings of the Buddha tell us of the fundamental unity of all things. This understanding is crucial if we are to take positive and decisive action on the pressing global concern with the environment.

"I believe all religions pursue the same goals, that of cultivating human goodness and bringing happiness to all human beings. Though the means might appear different the ends are the same.

"As we enter the final decade of this century I am optimistic that the ancient values that have sustained mankind are today reaffirming themselves to prepare us for a kinder, happier twenty-first century.

"I pray for all of us, oppressor and friend, that together we succeed in building a better world through human understanding and love, and that in doing so we may reduce the pain and suffering of all sentient beings. Thank you."

113

At the information office of the Dalai Lama in Dharamsala I had an opportunity to watch a video of the ceremony granting the prize, the festive dinner offered by the King of Norway, and a reindeer sleigh ride. The expression on the face of the God-king of Tibet when the sleigh moved in the snow behind the reindeer communicated exuberant joy. This part of the programme must have especially appealed to him.

For the Dalai Lama personally the Nobel Peace Prize did not mean very much, but he realised immediately that the granting of the award was of great importance for the Tibetans. He made it very clear in his speeches of thanks that the Tibetans were the real winners of the Nobel Peace Prize.

The Dalai Lama used the sum of money granted with the award for different humanitarian actions; the organization of the United Nations for Humanitarian and Economic Aid in Afghanistan, UNOCA, which was created at the beginning of 1990, received part of the monetary prize.

Support by Eastern Europe

"Small countries sometimes have the bigger heart", the Dalai Lama had told me when we talked in 1990 about the possibility of support from German-speaking countries such as Germany, Austria and Liechtenstein. In 1990 the Dalai Lama had visited Vaduz, the capital of Liechtenstein where Heinrich Harrer, who lived seven years in Tibet and who was one of the teachers of the young Dalai Lama, has his residence.

Our talk then focussed on possible support by the states of Eastern Europe which recently had gained independence. I asked the Dalai Lama if he could conceive of a political solution for Tibet analogous to the solutions for Namibia and Cambodia.

The Dalai Lama replied:

"Namibia, Cambodia and Tibet. I think, there are some similarities, but there are also some differences. The situation in Tibet can rather be compared with that of the Baltic States, even if those remained part of the Soviet Union for some time. They were annexed by force like Tibet. Tibet became part of China by force... There will remain perhaps a transition period of ten years."

I further asked whether, given the new dynamics of European engagement for Tibet, support would eventually come not from the West, but from Eastern Europe. The Dalai Lama replied: "This is possible. A special feeling results from having been oppressed. The people there had to suffer. It seems that this resulted in compassion for people in similar situations. I was in the GDR, in East Berlin (in the autumn of 1989) for about two hours, and then in Prague. In both cities I could feel the spontaneous, friendly sympathy of the population."

The Dalai Lama was especially impressed when he visited East Berlin on the precise day when Egon Krenz lost power. He visited the Wall. Observed by a "Vopo" (People's Police), he gave a red candle to an old woman. He lighted it and held it up high. At the beginning the flame flickered and seemed almost to die. But then it continued to burn. While he was surrounded by a crowd, and while people tried to approach the Dalai Lama to touch his hands, he prayed that the light of compassion and knowledge may fill the world and expel the darkness of fear and oppression. He writes in his autobiography that he never will forget this moment.

The former dissident Vaclav Havel invited the Dalai Lama as his first official guest immediately after becoming President of free Czechoslovakia which had gained independence from the Soviet Union. He was not deterred by all the protests from Peking. The reception offered to the Dalai Lama was magnificent. It was like being in Outer Mongolia, a close aide of the Dalai Lama mentioned. Tens of thousands gathered as if they wanted to experience receiving the benediction of the God-king of Tibet. Already at the airport hundreds of people waited, waving the Tibetan flag and shouting *tashi delek*, a Tibetan greeting which means "good luck".

The nonagenarian Cardinal Tomasek told the Dalai Lama that his visit was an honour for the population of Czechoslovakia.

The Dalai Lama gave a public lecture on Buddhism, followed by ten minutes of meditation. He not only held political talks with President Havel, but also informed him and some of his aides about the practice of Buddhist meditation.

In Wenzel Square the Dalai Lama prayed for the victims of oppression and injustice. A crowd demonstrated in front of the embassy of the People's Republic of China and demanded the independence of Tibet as well as an end to human rights violations.

On the invitation of President Vytautas Landsbergis the Dalai Lama visited Lithuania from the end of September to early October 1991.

He was the first official guest in the country which had recently gained independence.

In his speech the Dalai Lama praised the principles of struggle without violence, which had led to independence after fifty years of occupation by a foreign power. He mentioned that Lithuania could well serve as an inspiration to other nations, but also warned:

"During this critical period, fundamental principles must not be sacrificed on the grounds of expediency. Of particular importance is your continuing commitment to the principles of self-determination and non-violence."

He referred to the problems in Tibet: "We cannot free ourselves from this tyranny without the support of freedom-loving people outside Tibet."

Then he said that the success of Lithuania gave hope to the Tibetans that they also might be in the position to soon celebrate independence.

The Dalai Lama also visited Latvia at the invitation of President Anatolij Gorbunov. He spoke to deputies of the parliament in Riga and also delivered a speech in the university. He then visited Estonia where, however, he was not officially received, but had private talks with members of the parliament.

At the beginning of October, the Dalai Lama continued to travel for a state visit to Bulgaria, where he met President Schelju Schelew.

In February 1992, twenty nine Lithuanian members of parliament created a Parliamentary Support Group for Tibet.

In the statutes it is stipulated: "We recognize His Holiness the Dalai Lama and the Tibetan Government-in-Exile as the true representatives of the Tibetan Nation; we vow to support the legitimate aspirations of the Tibetan Nation in International Organizations and Fora."

As mentioned above, in May 1995 the second World Parliamentarians Conference was held in Vilnius, where it passed a significant resolution on Tibet, confirming that China has no valid legal title on Tibet and that Tibet is an occupied country.

Increasing Interest of Western States

In 1991, the Dalai Lama met President George Bush in Washington, D.C., and the British Prime Minister, John Major, in London.

A photograph of Prime Minister John Major at the side of the God-king of Tibet was then displayed resplendently in front of the holiest statue of Tibet in the Jokhang temple in Lhasa.

In spring of 1992, the Dalai Lama visited Australia and met Prime Minister Paul Keating in Canberra. In New Zealand he was received by Prime Minister James B. Bolger.

Later, in May 1992, the Dalai Lama visited South America. He went to Rio de Janeiro briefly before the beginning of the United Nations Global Conference on the Environment, which induced the Chinese Embassy to threaten that Prime Minister Li Peng would not attend the environmental summit until the Dalai Lama had departed. Nevertheless, the Brazilian President met the Dalai Lama, who also received the recognition of being appointed as an honorary citizen of Porto Alegre.

Then he was a guest of President Carlos Menem in Argentina and delivered lectures at the university of Buenos Aires and at the National University of Cordoba.

Visits to Chile and Venezuela followed.

This series of meetings of the God-king of Tibet with high officials must have worried Peking.

At the end of July 1992, the Dalai Lama was honorary

guest at the opening of the Salzburg Festival. He held talks with the Austrian President and the Chancellor. The newspapers reported the enthusiasm of the people at the beginning of the festival. "Here everything is perfect," the Dalai Lama said. "I cannot, however, forget, what is happening during these festivities in other parts of the world...

"We give too much importance to marginal things. If lunch arrives too late, or when a mosquito bites us, this is unpleasant. But what is the meaning of all this as compared to the incredible suffering, which people inflict on themselves!" His remarks concerning the terrible bloodshed in the successor states of Yugoslavia very much saddened his audience.

Many visits to Europe, the United States, Japan and — in 1994 for the first time — to the holy places of the Christians, Jews and Muslims in Jerusalem followed.

In 1995, President Bill Clinton talked with him in the White House in Washington D.C.

To the astonishment of some of his followers, newspapers reported about the presence of the God-king at two functions in different countries at the same time: The Dalai Lama met the Indian Ambassador in Tokyo in the afternoon of 14 April 1994 and had tea with the Governor of Hawaii in Honolulu the same afternoon. The mystery was revealed by the simple fact that he had crossed the international dateline in between the two engagements. The support of the Tibetan cause may, however, well require omnipresence.

Lhasa under Siege

Children of Tibet

TIBET'S STATUS ACCORDING TO INTERNATIONAL PUBLIC LAW

"To know, what you know,
And to know, what you do not know,
Only that means knowledge"
Confucius

The "Great Game", Tibet's Status and the Diplomacy of the Dalai Lama

In 1902, after the visit of the envoy of the XIII Dalai Lama, the Russian Minister of Foreign Affairs Count Lambsdorff tried appeasement: The contacts of his government with the Tibetans were only of religious nature and "could not be regarded as having political or diplomatic character".

What had happened? England harboured suspicions and had protested against the visit to Russia of the delegation of the Dalai Lama. After all, the Tsar had in June 1901 received an envoy of the God-king of Tibet, Agwan Dorzhiev, in his palace, accompanied by Lobsang Kaintchok Hambo.

Also the Tsarina, Maria Feodorovna, and of course Count Lambsdorff, himself received the Tibetan delegation.

The reason for the extreme British reaction was mistrust that Russia might wish to gain advantages in the "Great Game" played for control of Central Asia. Only three years later British troops commanded by Colonel Francis Younghusband marched into Tibet, destroying the fortress of Gyantse, the third largest city of Tibet and one of the most important trade centres for goods from Nepal and India. The British troops marched further and reached Lhasa. The Tibetan army was too weak to resist effectively.

The government of the Dalai Lama requested China to provide military assistance, basing the request on the Chö-Yön relationship. But China refused to live up to her commitment, being preoccupied because of the possibility of further confrontations with imperial England. The Dalai Lama fled. As a result of British urging the representative of the Chinese Emperor in Lhasa, the *Amban*, declared the Dalai Lama deposed.

The Tibetans ignored this declaration, which they considered absurd. Negotiations followed. In September of 1904 Younghusband as representative of England, the regent of the Dalai Lama, his cabinet and representatives of the three monastic universities Sera, Drepung and Ganden signed the so-called Lhasa Agreement. The British troops withdrew. This happened not least because of Russian pressure on the government in London.

From the viewpoint of international public law this British campaign at the beginning of the century has some interesting aspects: Not only did the "protecting power", China, protest against the invasion of Tibet — which was without doubt imperialist — but it remained Russia's privilege to vociferously protest against the violation of the rules of the "Great Game" by England. It becomes very evident that China had, at this time, no effective control over Tibet's territory. Peking was not even willing, or not in a position, to fulfill her obligation resulting from the Chö-Yön relationship — which corresponded to a kind of protectorate — and to grant military assistance against British aggression.

Eighty eight years after the consultations of Count Lambsdorff, the Russian Minister of Foreign Affairs, with the diplomatic emissaries of the XIII Dalai Lama in Saint Petersburg, another Count Lambsdorff — former Minister in the Federal Republic of Germany and Chairman of the Liberal Party — met the XIV Dalai Lama during a visit to Germany. He emphasized the need for conditions which are worthy of human beings in Tibet.

In his preface to a book on Tibet by the Italian journalist, Bruno Zoratto, published in 1990, he stresses:

"The Tibetan people suffered great injustice during the last decades. Partly because of the seclusion, partly because of opportunism in respect of the leaders in Peking, world public opinion which normally speaks with a loud voice, closed its eyes regarding this injustice... To the Chinese government, the fate of Honecker, Ceausescu or Noriega must appear like the writing on the wall."

Certainly, *raison d'état* made it necessary for the West to cultivate close relations with the People's Republic of China — especially in the era of the Cold War. China was indispensable to the framework of a strategy of containment against further Soviet expansion. With the peaceful liberation of Central and Eastern Europe, and with the collapse and the dissolution of the Soviet Union, however, the *raison-d'être* of this strategy of expansion ceased to exist. Special consideration in respect to the sensitivities of the present leadership in Peking does not seem to be opportune anymore, especially after the massacre on Tiananmen Square in Peking and after the supression of the democracy movement in China. Keeping in mind the possibility of a change in China, it may rather prove to be an advantage to have kept a distance from the present leadership.

Deserted his People?

The doyen of German experts on China, the former ambassador in Peking, Erwin Wickert, stated at a public hearing on Tibet, which had been convened by the Green Party under the chairmanship of Petra Kelly and Gert Bastian:

"...if I again may quote Confucius:

'To know, what you know
And to know, what you do not know
Only that means knowledge'

"Friends of the Dalai Lama often claim that the Chinese invaded and occupied the Tibetan state, and Mrs. Kelly and Mr. Alt have even compared it with the Soviet invasion of Afghanistan. Well, this comparison is inadmissible. International public law is a rational matter, free of emotions: Following criteria of international public law, for example, the Baltic States, which maintained relations with many states in the world and which were members of the League of Nations, were occupied by a foreign power. Tibet, however, is part of China, as Georgia is part of the Soviet Union. At most it could be compared with this republic of the USSR..."

"He who is silent...", as the old Latin proverb aptly says. Of course, Erwin Wickert could not foresee that Georgia would regain its full sovereignty within less than two years.

Tibetans, who had checked his words accurately, told me that they would not at all mind a "Georgian solution" for their country.

Former ambassador Wickert also insinuated at the hearing:

"The Dalai Lama fled from Tibet in 1959, because he was afraid to be taken prisoner by the Chinese after the aborted rebellion. He deserted his people, while the second highest spiritual leader of Tibet, the Panchen Lama, remained in the country and suffered severe persecution, — inter alia — imprisonment for sixteen years..."

The remark "he deserted his people" is palpably absurd, and may have been inspired by a close affinity of the author with Peking's propaganda. As to human rights, Erwin Wickert made the following remark at the hearing: "In China, where philosophical thoughts on politics have been current custom for more than 2,500 years, one has never spoken of human rights, but of human duties."

By March of 1992 his judgement on China had altered. He wrote in an article for the German daily newspaper, *Frankfurter Allgemeine Zeitung*: "Not we isolate China, it has isolated itself: with the massacres in Peking, and the ongoing rejection of the concepts of human rights in words and deeds, to which it was bound by becoming a member of United Nations...

"In Chinese history periods of strong central power have always alternated with periods during which the emperor was weak and the provinces went their own ways. Is such a change, favouring the provinces, now imminent? Or will they drift further apart, as during the years between the two world wars? Or will the empire break up as has happened several times in its long history?"

China without Legal Claim on Tibet

In 1989 the information office of the Dalai Lama in Dharamsala published three legal reports on the status of Tibet according to international public law. The publication contains one report from the lawyers Wilmer, Cutler and Pickering, dated 7 May 1986, the *Extract from the Report by the International Commission of Jurists' Legal Inquiry Committee on Tibet, 1960,* as well as a report from the Scientific Service of the German Federal Parliament, 1987.

All three reports express the view that Tibet was

from 1911-1912 until 1951 a fully sovereign state.

An additional reason in favour of this view is the fact that Tibet remained neutral during the Second World War, while China declared war against Germany.

A cable from Mao Zedong addressed to the X Panchen Lama in 1949, expressing his wish that Tibet should join the "motherland" China, is also of interest in this respect.

A state can only speak about the joining of another state, if this state is not yet part of its territory.

The United Kingdom had diplomatic relations with independent Tibet. After the independence of India in 1947, India took over the British mission in Lhasa. Nepal also maintained diplomatic relations with Tibet.

De facto, Tibet is today part of the Chinese state. This is a consequence of China's annexation of Tibet by force. Victims of this force were 1.2 million people who perished at Chinese hands or who died of hunger because they did not receive sufficient food during Mao's Great Leap Forward following the Chinese invasion.

Because the annexation of Tibet was by force, China could not acquire any valid legal title to Tibet. The Seventeen-Article Agreement between China and Tibet of 1951 especially does not provide a valid legal claim. This agreement was signed by the Tibetan delegation in Peking only under pressure, though the delegation did not carry the authority of the Tibetan Government. The fact, however, that the Tibetan Government made an effort until 1959 to keep to the respective regulations contained in the agreement, does not imply *de facto* recognition and hence the validity of the Seventeen-Article Agreement, because China did not honour her own obligations contained in the agreement, but violated them grossly. The agreement therefore has to be considered as invalid.

Nor did China gain legal title by usucapion. Such a title would presuppose that the Tibetan population agreed to the annexation and that there was no opposition to Chinese rule. Exactly the contrary is the case. Therefore usucapion is out of the question.

When, in the 1970s, the French President Giscard d'Estaing wanted to visit Lhasa following a visit to China, French diplomacy found an elegant formulation which avoided recognition of the illegal annexion of Tibet by China. After his departure from Peking, French newspapers announced that the president had left China and was on his way to Tibet. China felt obliged to protest formally, but Giscard had achieved his purpose of seeing Lhasa without antagonising the Tibetans and the world by acknowledging Chinese tyranny in Tibet.

THE PATH TO LIBERTY FOR TIBET

"Lack of freedom is like dew in the early morning, which vanishes when the first rays of the rising sun touch it."
  XIV Dalai Lama

Strategy for Tibet at the General Assembly of the United Nations and at the International Court of Justice

The Sub-Commission for Prevention of Discrimination and Protection of Minorities of the United Nations in Geneva in August 1991, for the first time, passed a resolution in which the violation of human rights in Tibet by China is condemned.

The Tibetan question was discussed by the General Assembly of the United Nations only in 1959, 1961 and 1965. Though in 1950 the representative of El Salvador at the United Nations, supported first by the delegations of India and the USA, had asked the General Assembly to hold a debate dealing with a request by Tibet concerning help against the Chinese aggression. In the appeal of the Tibetans it was said:

"We can assure you, Mr. Secretary-General, that Tibet will not vanish without a fight. Although there is little hope that a nation which has lived dedicated to peace will be able to resist the brutal efforts of men who have been trained for war, we have the knowledge that the United Nations are committed to stop aggressions wherever they occur."

Unfortunately the Tibetan Government had erred in the assumption that the United Nations would be ready, under the obligation contained in their Charter, to stop the foreign aggression by China.

Two days before the appeal Communist Chinese forces had also intervened in Korea; consequently attention turned away from Tibet. On the day when the Tibetan request was considered, General MacArthur launched a military offensive in Korea. The Indian Government wanted to mediate between China and the

United States and the representative of India at the United Nations convinced his own government that India's support for El Salvador's proposal for a debate could eventually impede those efforts for mediation as well as possible mediation by India in the conflict between China and Tibet. The British representative as well as the representative of the United States agreed to this view. Tibet was not put on the agenda of the General Assembly.

In 1959 Malaya and Ireland requested the General Assembly to discuss the question of Tibet. In 1961 Ireland, Malaya, Thailand and El Salvador again brought the question of Tibet to the General Assembly; then again in 1965, when Nicaragua and the Philippines associated themselves with the above states. The resolutions adopted by the United Nations criticize the Chinese policy and the violation of human rights in Tibet.

Certainly, now would be the right moment for states which are friendly towards Tibet to endeavour to have this question, and especially the status of Tibet, discussed in the General Assembly.

The Central and Eastern European states, which only recently liberated themselves from Communist oppression, may show a special readiness to request the General Assembly to discuss the economic and social conditions and the status of Tibet.

If the Chinese Government were to protest and raise the objection that the question of Tibet was an "internal matter" of the People's Republic of China, the legitimate government of Tibet and the states, which support the demand of Tibet, could ask the International Court in The Hague to prepare a judicial opinion concerning Tibet's legal status. Such expertise would almost certainly have to conclude that the occupation and annexation of Tibet was illegal, that China had committed genocide, and that finally — because Tibet never accepted foreign rule, even after 1959 — China did not acquire a legal title to Tibet.

When the question of Tibet is considered by the General Assembly, world attention would certainly focus again on Tibet. Hence the Chinese Government could be moved to seek a compromise by accepting talks with the Government-in-Exile of the Dalai Lama, and finally to accept the 1987 Five-point Peace Plan of the Dalai Lama.

If the Chinese Government, however, were not ready for compromise, the states supporting the legitimate government of Tibet could demand in the General Assembly that Tibet be provisionally put under a United Nations mandate, following the example of Namibia and Cambodia. In line with the latter example, the sovereignty of Tibet would be assumed during a transitional period by the United Nations, until the Tibetan people could exercise their right to self-determination through free elections.

As in the case of the illegal occupation of Cambodia until the Agreement of Paris in October 1991 to a political solution, and as in the case of Afghanistan until the departure of Soviet troops in 1989, the General Assembly of United Nations could adopt annual resolutions concerning Tibet. The essence of such a resolution should consist of a demand for the withdrawal of Chinese troops and the right of the Tibetan people to self-determination.

Without a doubt such resolutions would exercise a degree of pressure on China to work towards an understanding which would be satisfactory for the Tibetans.

132

To oppose Tibet's spiritual dynamism, based on an invincible longing for freedom, the Chinese leadership can muster nothing other than brute force, relying on the barrels of guns.

Assisted by freedom-loving peoples around the world, and with the commitment of their governments at the General Assembly, the efforts to ensure Tibet's liberty could succeed.

Chances after the End of Communist Rule in China?

How will the situation for Tibet change if there really is a new situation in China, if the communist regime in Peking does dissolve itself or if it is overthrown?

Yan Jiaqi, Chairman of the "Federation for Democracy in China", an association of leaders of the Chinese democracy movement who were able to escape from China after the massacre on Tiananmen Square, said during a press conference in Paris in September 1989:

"We will be happy if the Dalai Lama sends his representatives. The representatives of the Dalai Lama will come to our press conference. Our cause is the same as theirs. The democratic cause concerns every Chinese who lives in China, the Tibetans, Han and also the people of Hongkong, Taiwan and everywhere.

"During the preparation for this conference we discussed the Tibetan question several times. We already have an opinion on the subject. We would like to say that the term of "counter-revolutionary rebellions" in reference to the events in 1959 and 1989 will be corrected, and we hope that this can be discussed. The resistance of the Tibetan people against the dictatorship of the Communist Party was the right thing to do. One of the goals of our Federation is to have human rights respected in China, everywhere in China, including Tibet of course, and of course, it means the right to believe in whatever religion one wants to believe.

"One must respect the freedom of religion and the freedom not to believe in religion. Our democratic China will have a new system, as a United States of China or as a Federation... I personally think that the solution to the Tibetan problem could be the solution of a federation.

"The Dalai Lama has been in exile for thirty years; we must express our admiration for his continuing struggle for a better situation in Tibet."

It is remarkable that the leader of the democracy movement should adopt a conciliatory attitude towards Tibet and recognise the right to self-determination of the Tibetan people, respectively the right to be connected with China only in a federation. They therefore distinguish themselves not only from the political attitude of the present leadership in Peking, but also from that of the Kuomintang under Chiang Kai-shek.

The Concept of the Dalai Lama for the Future of Tibet

In September 1991 the God-king of Tibet withdrew his proposal to the European Parliament in Strasbourg, in which he had not asked for the full independence of Tibet, but declared himself satisfied with the real autonomy of his country.

In a conversation in December 1991 the Dalai Lama explained to me his new concept for the future of Tibet.

Now, after twelve years of utmost efforts to find an arrangement — which, regardless of which terms are applied, could have been a kind of highest autonomy for Tibet — it has become evident, that these efforts have not succeeded. This has been caused by China's attitude.

The Dalai Lama remarked in this respect:

"During the first direct contacts the Chinese Government showed willingness for concessions. The Chinese declared their readiness to talk about everything, except full independence of Tibet."

On this basis he had continued his efforts on behalf of Tibet over the past twelve years. Peking had only pretended to hold negotiations on Tibet. In the meantime, his approach of compromise with China received much criticism everywhere in the world.

"Now, after twelve years of vain efforts, I have no other choice than to try to gain independence. In practice I believe it will be self-determination."

At this stage he would be obliged to wait for a new situation to arise in China. He did not believe, however, that China could learn from the events in the Soviet Union. No, the present China did not learn at all. The leaders of China were proud; they even believed that they could give a lesson to the Russians. His present strategy, which had been set out in a recently completed document, was as follows:

"When I return in freedom, my first task will be to hold elections and appoint a new government. Elections have to take place on the basis of a democratic electoral system. This government will be an interim government.

Once the government is appointed, I will hand over all my authority. I will become an ordinary citizen.

Then the government should at once hold elections for a constituent assembly. The constitution, which has to be finalised, should — if possible — be secular. In reality the majority of Tibetans are Buddhists, though there are several thousand Muslims and about 100,000 followers of the traditional religion, which is not formally Buddhism. Therefore the government of the nation has to be based on secularism...

"The economy will be organised in accordance with the system of a mixed economy. The government will most probably have a parliamentarian system and will be — of course — completely demilitarised. My aim is to have such a constitution. If it has been formally accepted, there will have to be elections again according to the constitution, by which the majority of the voters will elect the government.

"This is a way, a kind of strategy to follow."

Hence the future system of government of Tibet should not have theocratic patterns, as in the time of his former rule, according to the wishes of the Dalai Lama.

An example for him would rather be the system of liberal democracy with separation of power and political participation by representatives of the people, chosen in free elections.

On 10 March 1992, the thirty third anniversary of the uprising against Chinese oppression of Tibet, the Dalai Lama made a speech which shows the way to be followed:

"... I am more optimistic than ever before about the future of Tibet. This optimism stems from the determination of the Tibetan people inside Tibet, and also from the dramatic changes that have taken place everywhere in the world, particularly in the erstwhile Soviet Union. I feel certain that within the next five to ten years some major changes will take place in China. The collapse of totalitarian regimes in different parts of the world, the break-up of the Soviet empire and the re-emergence of sovereign, independent nations reinforce our belief in the ultimate triumph of truth, justice and the human spirit. The bloody October Revolution of 1917, which controlled the fate of the Soviet Union for seven decades, came to an end in the bloodless, non-violent August Revolution of 1991.

"We know from history that the mightiest of empires and military powers come and go. No power remains sacrosanct for ever. This is particularly true in this modern age when the power of communication is so effective. It is, therefore, quite clear that China cannot remain unaffected by what is happening inside and outside the country...

"The present Chinese leadership today has two choices. The first one is to start an enlightened political process for a smooth transition towards a fully democratic society and allow the countries they have forcibly annexed and occupied to become free and equal partners in a new world order. The second choice is to push the country to the brink of bloody political struggles, which in a country populated by a quarter of humanity would be a great tragedy. On our part, there will be no lack of willingness or sincerity, should the Chinese Government show a genuine interest in finding a solution to the Tibetan problem. Even though the Strasbourg Proposal, which I made more than three years ago, is no longer valid, we are committed to the path of negotiations. This willingness is amply demonstrated in my proposal for an early visit to Tibet.

Regrettably, this proposal was turned down by the Chinese government...

"The unique feature of our struggle has been its non-violent nature. While we continue to strive for our legitimate rights, we must not deviate from the path of non-violence. I have no doubt that one day our people, as well as the peoples of Inner Mongolia and East Turkestan will be reunited in full freedom in their respective countries...

"When a genuinely cordial relationship is established between the Tibetans and the Chinese, it will enable us not only to resolve the disputes between our two nations in this century, but will also enable the Tibetans to make a significant contribution through our rich cultural tradition for mental peace among millions of young Chinese."

This last sentence of the speech concerning the "spiritual and mental peace" of millions of young Chinese seems especially important. Because of the spiritual vacuum after the break-down of the pretention to the ideology of Marxism-Leninism and the thoughts of Mao Zedong, many young people are without orientation. There is a lack of values. The main objectives focus on material matters.

Peking reacted angrily to the speech. It decided to launch an attack and accused the Dalai Lama immediately after the speech of wanting to reunite the "three Mongolias", Outer Mongolia, Inner Mongolia and the area of the settlement of the Mongolian Buryats in Siberia (the region near Ulan Ude and Chita, note by the author). The leadership in Peking must be aware that it cannot offer anything to the youth in respect to "spiritual leadership" and that, therefore, the foundations of the People's Republic of China could soon tremble.

Inspite of all the desperation of Tibetans in an ever-worsening situation for them in Tibet, due to an increasing transfer of Chinese settlers into their land, and in view of the escalating systematic destruction of Tibetan culture by the Chinese, the Dalai Lama maintained his policy of the "Middle-Way Approach". When I met him in June 1995 in Dharamsala, to discuss the Tibetan policy for an imminent hearing on Tibet by the German Parliament, the Dalai Lama emphasized that, inspite of direct contacts with the Chinese over fifteen years, and his wish to bring about such negotiations with the Chinese, there had been no progress at all. Because of his efforts to have such negotiations, however, he felt he would have had difficulties in raising the issue of Tibet at the same time before the General Assembly of the United Nations.

Now, because the situation inside Tibet has deteriorated rapidly, he favoured pressure on China by as many statements as possible issued by friendly countries.

He felt very encouraged, however, by the example of the Tribunal in the Hague, which has been given a mandate by the United Nations to investigate the genocide in Bosnia; he sees this as a means for the international community to take action when illegal aggression occurs.

His idea was not to raise the question of the independence of Tibet. He was convinced that it would be possible to find a satisfactory solution for Tibet simultaneously with the improvement of the situation in China.

The Dalai Lama pointed out that in the past only Tibet has had a special agreement with the government in Peking, not the provinces of China. Zhou Enlai had informed the Indian Prime Minister that he considered Tibet not to be an ordinary province of China. Contrary to the opinion of certain governments, the media in the entire world considered Tibet to be an occupied country.

His main goal was the preservation of Tibetan culture. He asked for understanding that – since a large part of the Tibetan people lived in regions which previously belonged to Tibet – his efforts for the preservation of Tibetan culture could not exclude those Tibetans.

There is evidence that the present government in China is getting increasingly nervous about statements by parliaments and governments around the world asking Peking to engage in negotiations towards real autonomy for Tibet with the Dalai Lama. This nervousness was reflected in Chinese reactions before and after the brief meeting of President Clinton with the Dalai Lama in The White House in September 1995.

There is, however, no reason why the present or future Chinese leaders should not reconsider their current stand and adopt a wise policy for the greater benefit of all people who are presently under China's control. Any government in Peking will have to try to win back its status as a respected member of the international community. This can only be achieved if the huge shadows of genocide, oppression and cultural destruction in Tibet vanish.

Today there is no geo-political reason which would obstruct a change in the Chinese policy towards Tibet: At the time of the threat to Communist China by the United States of America, from 1949 till rapprochement in 1972, control of Tibet was of significant importance for China. After the break with the Soviet Union at the beginning of the sixties, and the war with India in 1962, China had enemies also in the north, the west, and the

140

south. With the dissolution of the Soviet Union in 1991 no new threat to China can be perceived. The meeting of President Yelzin and the Presidents of Kasachstan, Kyrgisia and Tajikistan with the Chinese leadership in Shanghai in April 1996 resulted in the signature of agreements on mutual reductions of troops at the former border of the Soviet Union and China. An era of detente has emerged. Hence a new orientation of China's security policy seems to be timely. It does not make much sense for China to continue its colonial policy towards Tibet, and therefore be considered an enemy by the Tibetans, and hence be always accused by world opinion of violation of human rights in Tibet.

On 6 October 1991, on the seventy fourth anniversary of the October Revolution in Russia, the Communist Party was dissolved in Russia, and on 25 December 1991 the Soviet Union disintegrated.

Did Peking see the writing on the wall?

The statement of Dalai Lama on 10 March 1996 is another genuine attempt to settle differences with the Chinese Government on friendly terms to end the suffering of the Tibetans. He states that a transformation from the current regime in Peking into one which is more open, free and democratic is inevitable. (See Annex II)

The Dalai Lama once said that lack of freedom is like the dew in the early morning that vanishes when the first rays of the rising sun touch it.

The spiritual force of Tibetan Buddhism, the radiation of the spirit of the Tibetans, and their uncompromising longing for liberty seem to indicate that there is hope for Tibet.

There are further indications that also for China the beginning of the final end of communism is already underway. The spiritual fight for liberty in Tibet could soon prove to be — just as the inscription on the small Tibetan coin, which the Dalai Lama gave to me during an audience in Dharamsala, suggests — victorious in all directions.

ANNEX I

The following is an extract from the text of the X Panchen Lama's address to the 'TAR' Standing Committee Meeting of the National People's Congress held in Peking on 28 March 1987

The government's work report and other related matters presented by Prime Minister Zhao Ziyang was received with great appreciation by everyone, and I fully support that.

It is good to speak on all aspects of our country. The policy directions charted by the Third Meeting of the Eleventh Session of the CPC Central Committee were appropriate to the reality of our country. I have no doubt that these will help improve our efficiency and ensure good results...

Ours is a country of many nationalities. Apart from the Chinese, there are fifty five nationalities, which are in the minority. The leftist trend before, and especially after the time of the Cultural Revolution, has caused the minorities to suffer in many ways. Just recently, a story, entitled *Pasang and Her Relátives*, was intentionally published in a journal to ridicule the Tibetans. Last year our representatives from Tibet raised their objection to this story when it was a film script. We even asked Vice-Chairman Ngabo Ngawang Jigme to express our misgiving about this story to the concerned departments. However, there has been no response. Instead, the film, was awarded a first prize. Another film of this nature, entitled *Compassion Without Mercy*, was also given an award. Things like this have been done to other nationalities as well.

In November, last year, a ten-point legal document

was circulated with an instruction that we should study it. But this document was silent on the subject of the regional autonomy of minority areas. During the Twentieth Session of the Standing Committee of the National People's Congress, we asked the law department how such an important matter was left out of this document. The response was that the study of the laws relating to the governance of autonomous regions should be left to the respective minority nationalities...

I strongly objected to this by stating that it should be studied also by the Chinese and especially by the officials, who are in a position to implement it. "It is not that we are not able to exercise power, but that we have not been given any power. A servant is naked not because he does not want to wear clothes, but because his master has not given him any clothes," I said...

At the time of the liberation, Mao Zedong and Zhou Enlai proceeded in consultation with concerned nationalities. But what has become of the status of nationalities since then is something I cannot understand. I hope everybody will try to understand it.

Although the minority nationalities constitute only about six percent of the Chinese population, they own sixty four percent of Chinese territory. Therefore, it is in the interest of China to ensure that there is peace and stability in these regions...

During my visit to Kham last year, I noticed a great deal of devastation caused by large-scale and indiscriminate deforestation. I saw huge landslides caused by this. Industries with the potential to generate high revenue are closed down in minority regions. To take an example, there was a cigarette factory in Taklo-Tron, Yunnan, which could be very profitable. But this factory had to be closed down because of a shortage of trained manpower and the poor quality cigarettes it produced. This despite the fact that it was using high-quality raw materials. The industries in Shanghai, on the other hand, do not use high-quality raw materials, but they have trained personnel and the best possible technology, resulting in high-quality goods and profit.

What Ringzin Wangyal said regarding the handling of unrest in Tibet was quite true. In 1959 there were rebellions in Tibet. Forces were despatched to quell the disorder, which was a right decision and should not be gainsaid. However, a lot innocent people were also persecuted. Many mistakes were made in the way the crack-down operations were mounted. The authorities did not make any distinction between those guilty and not guilty of participation in the disturbance. People were arrested and jailed indiscriminately. There were no interrogations. On sight Tibetans were taken to jail and beaten. Things like this are still commonplace in Tibet. This is very sad and there is still widespread resentment among the people. We should consider this as a serious matter. We should examine and investigate these practices and bring the guilty to book. This is the way by which we will be able to assuage people's resentment. Isn't this what we are here to discuss?

In the past, I was punished for submitting a 70,000-character petition. I had clearly mentioned these facts in that petition. In fact, I said the same thing as Ngabo about the way senior officials of the former local government of Tibet functioned. They had a well-established structure and legal system. The aristocrats, who were members of the government, were banished, wearing a white *chuba* (Tibetan garment) and riding a red ox, if they failed to carry out the instructions of the government. What would you do if this sort of thing happened to you? A career is important to everyone.

In the Seventeen-Point Agreement, it was emphatically stated that there would be no change in the power of the Tibetan local government until the introduction of democratic reforms. The same promise was made to the Tashi Lhunpo monastic authorities. However, what happened later could be summed up by this dictum: "Critising the old system from the perspective of a new ideology." This kind of practice is not very ethical. A scientist must arrive at his decision according to whatever is proved right scientifically. The Tibetan aristocrats had served the government for generations. They were deeply devoted to the Dalai Lama and turned to him for refuge both in this and the next life. This is an undeniable fact. Later on, however, the aristocrats were accused of being the leaders of the rebellions and persecuted. This, I think, was an absolutely wrong thing to do. I had clearly recorded these facts in my petition. Of course, I was criticised and punished for this. But truth is timeless. It always remains the same. Undoubtedly, these were mistakes in my petition. But I have never been wrong in speaking up. The mistakes in the content of my petition are mistakes, both today and in the past. But there should be a clear dividing line spelling out where I went wrong and where I was right...

Talking about Lhoka, first the Khampa guerrillas were based there. But when the Dalai Lama passed through there, people happily donated butter, barley flour and other provisions without being asked. This was, of course, a spontaneous gesture of love by the people. Later on, the people who served them were treated as active members of the resistance. How can you do such a thing? This is something that everyone should know. Speaking about myself, those days whenever I passed by, people would show love and devotion to me. Now should this be construed as a politically motivated act? Amongst other things, they showed respect to me because they were religious-minded and it is a Tibetan custom. Due care and consideration must be shown to customs and traditions that are special to Tibet.

Quelling the rebellions and introducing reforms was right in principle. But there was a strong leftist tinge to the way these were done. Such things should not happen again and they must be rectified. During the last three decades of communist rule, there have been many good things done and many bad things also. These were considered in the sixth meeting of the Eleventh National Congress of CPC, and were publicised internationally. Owning up to our mistakes will not damage the Party's image; rather it would help build it. Speaking about the former comrades in the Tibet Military Command Centre and the Chengdu Military Command Centre, some comrades told me that they should not have done what they did. This was a healthy attitude. We frequently say that great achievements were made with your sweat in the liberation and reformation of Tibet and that the people of Tibet will never forget this. This is an honest statement. However, you did make a great deal of mistakes, and these also in Tibet. These too, we will never forget. What I am saying is for the purpose of rectifying these mistakes. If we can do this, we can make progress. I am saying this with the best of intentions.

I will tell you a more personal story at this point. The Government of the Kashag spearheaded the rebellion. Those of us at the *Labrangs* (Monastic institutions)

147

were not a party to any agitation. In the beginning, we were told great things about peaceful reforms and policies of fraternal relations. However, when the reforms were undertaken, people belonging to our establishment were subjected to untold sufferings. This filled people with disgust and disbelief. Most of the members of the local Tibetan government fled from Tibet. A handful, who stayed back, were praised and appointed to government jobs as shining examples of a progressive element. Our people who stayed back in solidarity with China were subjected to unthinkable sufferings. Being in Lhasa, as I was at that time, I did not suffer so much. But all my family members were subjected to *Thamzing* (Public Struggle Sessions).

There was one woman, a wife of one of my staff, who was also arrested. One day, when she was called into the interrogation chamber, she muttered, "This man called Panchen has caused me so much suffering that I will die of depression." This utterance led the authorities into believing that she would say something incriminating about me. This was a much-awaited chance for the authorities to take up punitive measures against me. They immediately called the scribes to record her testimony. Then she went on, "We made a big mistake by following this man called Panchen and not participating in the fight against the Chinese. If he had led us in rebellion against the Chinese, our condition today would be much better than this. Because, initially, we would have killed as many Chinese as possible and then fled to India. Our people, both men and women, are being persecuted here. We are experiencing hell on earth."

If there was a film made on all the atrocities perpetrated in Qinghai province, it would shock the viewers. In Golok area, many people were killed and their dead bodies were rolled down the hill into a big ditch. The soldiers told the family members and relatives of the dead people that they should all celebrate since the rebels had been wiped out. They were even forced to dance on the dead bodies. Soon after, they were also massacred with machine guns. They were all buried there.

Actually, the rebellions did not occur in all these areas. In Kham, of course, there were rebellions in many places. In Jharoong Parpo and Mili, both in Amdo, the nomads collected their guns and gave them over to the Chinese authorities. They were praised and garlanded during a special function. After the function, they were driven to their villages where they were immediately arrested and imprisoned for a long time. There were some very old people among them. In Amdo and Kham, people were subjected to unspeakable atrocities. People were shot in groups of ten or twenty. I know that it is not good to speak about these things. But such actions have left deep wounds in the minds of the people. There are some officials who always leave behind a bad legacy. What is the purpose of doing this? The guilty must, of course, be punished. But what is the use of leaving behind a bad legacy. People who persist in doing this are really stupid. But there are some who consider these people very wise and capable. Comrade Wu Jinhua has a plan to investigate the methods and mistakes made by some of the officials in putting down the Tibetan rebellion. I feel this investigation needs to be done with the utmost diligence.

In Qinghai, for example, there are between one to three or four thousand villages and towns, each having between three to four thousand families with four to five thousand people. From each town and village, about 800 to 1,000 people were imprisoned. Out of this, at least 300 to 400 people of them died in prison. This means almost half of the prison population perished. Last year, we discovered that only a handful of people had participated in the rebellion. Most of these people were completely innocent. In my 70,000-character petition, I mentioned that about five percent of the population had been imprisoned. According to my information at that time, it was between ten to fifteen percent. But I did not have the courage to state such a huge figure. I would have died under *Thamzing* (Public Struggle Session) If I had stated the real figure. These are serious matters as far as Tibet is concerned. If we pay only lip service to these kind of mistakes and do nothing to redress them, there will be equally serious consequences. People may not like what I am saying. But I am saying this out of my love for the motherland.

In 1964, when I was called to Peking, some leaders told me, "You are turning against the motherland. Are you trying to start a secessionist rebellion? Even if the whole of the Tibetan population is armed, it will only make over three million people. We are not scared of this." On hearing this, I felt very sad and realised how it is to be without freedom.

Statement of His Holiness the Dalai Lama on the Thirty Seventh Anniversary of Tibetan National Uprising Day.

As we commemorate today the thirty seventh anniversary of the Tibetan people's national uprising, we are witnessing a general hardening of Chinese government policy. This is reflected in an increasingly aggressive posture towards the peoples of Taiwan and Hong Kong and in intensified repression in Tibet. We also see rising fear and suspicion throughout the Asia-Pacific region and a worsening of relations between China and much of the rest of the world.

Within the context of this tense political atmosphere, Peking has once again sought to impose its will on the Tibetan people by appointing a rival Panchen Lama. In doing so, it has chosen a course of total disregard both for the sentiments of the Tibetans in general and for Tibetan spiritual tradition in particular, despite my every effort to reach for some form of understanding and cooperation with the Chinese Government. Significantly, the official Chinese media compare the present political climate in Tibet with that in Poland during the Solidarity years of the 1980's. This demonstrates a growing sense of insecurity on the part of the Chinese leadership as a result of which, through a continuing campaign of coercion and intimidation, Peking has greatly reinforced its repression throughout Tibet. I am therefore saddened to have to report that the situation of our people in Tibet continues to deteriorate.

Nevertheless, it remains my strong conviction that

change for the better is coming. China is at a critical junction: its society is undergoing profound changes and the country's leadership is facing the transition to a new generation. It is obvious too that the Tiananmen massacre has failed to silence the call for freedom, democracy and human rights in China. Moreover, the impressive democratization in process across the Taiwan Strait must further invigorate the democratic aspirations of the Chinese people. Indeed, Taiwan's historic first direct presidential elections later this month are certain to have an immense political and psychological impact on their minds. A transformation from the current totalitarian regime in Peking into one which is more open, free and democratic is thus inevitable. The only outstanding question is how and when and whether the transition will be a smooth one.

As a human being, it is my sincere desire that our Chinese brothers and sisters enjoy freedom, democracy, prosperity and stability. As a Buddhist monk, I am of course concerned that a country which is home to almost a quarter of the world's entire population and which is on the brink of an epic change, should undergo that change peacefully. In view of China's huge population, chaos and instability could lead to large-scale bloodshed and tremendous suffering for millions of people. Such a situation would also have serious ramifications for peace and stability throughout the world. As a Tibetan, I recognize that the future of our country and our people depends to a great extent on what happens in China during the years ahead.

Whether the coming change in China brings new life and new hope for Tibet and whether China herself emerges as a reliable, peaceful and constructive member of the international community depends to a large degree on the extent to which the international community itself adopts responsible policies towards China. I have always drawn attention to the need to bring Peking into the mainstream of world democracy and have spoken against any idea of isolating and containing China. To attempt to do so would be morally incorrect and politically impractical. Instead, I have always counselled a policy of responsible and principled engagement with the Chinese leadership.

It became obvious during the Tiananmen movement that the Chinese people yearn for freedom, democracy, equality and human right no less than any other people. Moreover, I was personally very moved to see that those young people, despite being taught that "political power comes out of the barrel of a gun" pursued their aims without resorting to violence. I, too, am convinced that non-violence is the appropriate way to bring about constructive political change.

Based on my belief in non-violence and in dialogue, I have consistently tried to engage the Chinese government in serious negotiations concerning the future of the Tibetan people. In order to find a mutually acceptable solution, I have adopted a 'middle-way' approach. This is also in response to, and within the frame-work of, Mr. Deng Ziaoping's stated assurance that "anything except independence can be discussed and resolved". Unfortunately, the Chinese Government's response to my many overtures has been consistently negative. But, I remain confident that his successors will realize the wisdom of resolving the problem of Tibet through dialogue.

The Tibet issue will neither go away of its own accord, nor can it be wished away. As the past has clearly shown, neither intimidation nor coercion of the

Tibetan people can force a solution. Sooner or later, the leadership in Peking will have to face this fact. Actually, the Tibet problem represents an opportunity for China. If it were solved properly through negotiation, not only would it be helpful in creating a political atmosphere conducive to the smooth transition of China into a new era but also China's image throughout the world would be greatly enhanced. A properly negotiated settlement would furthermore have a strong, positive impact on the peoples of both Hong Kong and Taiwan and will do much to improve Sino-Indian relations by inspiring genuine trust and confidence.

For our part, we seek to resolve the issue of Tibet in a spirit of reconciliation, compromise and understanding. I am fully committed to the spirit of the 'middle-way approach'. We wish to establish a sustainable relationship with China based on mutual respect, mutual benefit and friendship. In doing so, we will think not only about the fundamental interests of the Tibetan people, but also take seriously the consideration of China's security concerns and her economic interests. Moreover, if our Buddhist culture can flourish once again in Tibet, we are confident of being able to make a significant contribution to millions of our Chinese brothers and sisters by sharing with them those spiritual and moral values which are so clearly lacking in China today.

Despite the absence of positive and conciliatory gestures from the Chinese Government to my initiatives, I have always encouraged Tibetans to develop personal relationships with Chinese. I make it a point to ask the Tibetans to distinguish between the Chinese people and the policies of the totalitarian government in Peking.

I am thus happy to observe that there has been significant progress in our efforts to foster closer interaction amongst the people of our two communities, mainly between exile Tibetans and Chinese living abroad. Moreover, human rights activitists and democrats within China, people like the brave Wei Jingsheng, are urging their leaders to respect the basic human rights of the Tibetan people and pledging their support of our rights to self-rule. Chinese scholars outside China are discussing a constitution for a federated China which envisages a confederal status for Tibet. These are most encouraging and inspiring developments. I am, therefore, very pleased that the people-to-people dialogue between the Tibetans and Chinese is fostering a better understanding of our mutual concerns and interests.

In recent years we have also witnessed the growth of a world-wide grass-roots movement in support of our non-violent struggle for freedom. Reflecting this, many governments and parliaments have come forward with strong expressions of concern and support for our efforts. Notwithstanding the immediate negative reactions of the Chinese regime, I strongly believe that such expressions of international support are essential. They are vital in communicating a sense of urgency to the minds of leadership in Peking and in helping persuade them to negotiate.

I would like to take this opportunity to thank the numerous individuals, also the members of governments, of parliaments, of non-governmental organizations and of religious orders who have supported my appeal for the safety and freedom of the young Panchen Lama, Gedhun Choekyi Nyima. I am grateful for their continued intervention and efforts on behalf of this

155

child who must be the world's youngest political prisoner. I also wish to thank our supporters all over the world who are commemorating today's anniversary of the Tibetan people's uprising with peaceful activities in every part of the globe. I urge the Chinese Government not to construe such support for Tibet as anti-Chinese. The purpose and aim of these activities is to appeal to the Chinese leadership and people to recognize the legitimate rights of the Tibetan people.

In conclusion, I am happy to state today that our exile community's experiment in democracy is progressing well without any major setbacks or difficulties. Last autumn, the Tibetans in exile participated in preliminary polls to nominate candidates for the Twelfth Assembly of the Tibetan People's Deputies, the parliament in exile. Next month, they return to the polls to elect the members themselves. This accords with my conviction that democracy is the best guarantee for the survival and future of the Tibetan people. Democracy entails responsibilities as well as rights. The success of our struggle for freedom will therefore depend directly on our ability to shoulder these collectively. It is thus my hope that the Twelfth Assembly will emerge as a united, mature and dedicated representation of our people. This will ultimately depend on every franchised member of our community. Each one is called upon to cast his or her vote with an informed and unbiased mind, with a clear awareness of the need of the hour and with a strong sense of individual responsibility.

With my homage to the brave men and women of Tibet, who have died for the cause of our freedom, I pray for an early end to the suffering of our people.

SELECTED BIBLIOGRAPHY

ENGLISH BOOKS

Charles Allen, *A Mountain in Tibet,* London 1982

George Allen, *The Way of Power, a Practical Guide to the Tantric Mysticism of Tibet,* London 1970

John F. Avedon, *In Exile from the Land of Snows,* London 1979

Sir Charles Bell, *Portrait of the Dalai Lama,* London 1946

Dalai Lama, *The Union Of Bliss And Emptiness,* New York 1988

Dalai Lama. *Freedom in Exile, The Autobiography of His Holiness The Dalai Lama of Tibet,* London 1990

Dalai Lama, *Universal Responsibility and the Environment, California University Press, 1989.*

Alexandra David-Neel, *My Journey To Lhasa,* First Edition, 1927, reprinted London 1983

Alexandra David-Neel, *Magic and Mystery in Tibet,* London 1965

Vanya Kewley, *Tibet Behind the Ice Curtain,* London 1990

Ram Rahul, *The Government and Politics of Tibet,* Delhi 1969

Ram Rahul, *Politics of Central Asia,* Delhi 1974

Amaury de Riencourt, *Lost World Tibet,* updated edition, England 1987

Tsepon W. D. Shakabpa, *Tibet: A Political History,* First Printing, USA, 1967

Tibetan Young Buddhist Association, *Tibet The Facts,* Second Revised Edition, Dharamsala 1990

Michael C.van Walt van Praag, *The Status of Tibet. History, Rights, and Prospects in International Law,* Boulder 1987

ENGLISH JOURNALS

The Tibet Journal, ed. by Library of Tibetan Works and Archives, Dharamsala

Tibetan Bulletin, ed. by The Department of Information and International Relations, Central Tibetan Secretariat, Dharamsala

GERMAN BOOKS

Catriona Bass, *Der Ruf des Muschelhorns, Begegnung mit Tibet,* Reinbek bei Hamburg 1992

Dalai Lama, *Das Auge der Weisheit, Grundzüge der buddhistischen Lehre für den westlichen Leser,* Bern 1975

Lama Anagarika Govinda, *Der Weg der Weißen Wolken*, Zürich 1969

Heinrich Harrer, *Sieben Jahre in Tibet*, Frankfurt/Main 1952

Heinrich Harrer, *Wiedersehen mit Tibet*, Innsbruck 1983

Petra K. Kelly, Gert Bastian (Hg), *Tibet - ein vergewaltigtes Land*, Reinbek bei Hamburg 1988

Petra K. Kelly, Gert Bastian (Hg), *Tibet klagt an, Zur Lage in einem besetzten Land*, Wuppertal 1990

Helmut Uhlig, *Tibet, Ein verbotenes Land öffnet seine Tore*, Bergisch Gladbach 1986

Helmut Uhlig, *Himalaya, Menschen und Kulturen in der Heimat des Schnees*, Bergisch Gladbach 1987

E. Schlagintweit, *Die Könige von Tibet von der Entstehung königlicher Macht in Yarlung bis zum Erlöschen in Ladak*, Munich 1866

E. Schlagintweit, *Die Lebensbeschreibung von Padma Sambhava, dem Begründer des Lamaismus 747 n.Chr.Teil I:Die Vorgeschichte*, München 1899; Teil II:Wirken und Erlebnisse in Indien. In:Abh.d. Königl. bayer.Akademie der Wissenschaften,XXII,S.519-576

Albert Schweitzer, *Die Weltanschauung der indischen Denker*, Nachdruck 1987 der dritten, auf Grund der englischen Ausgabe von 1935 neugefaßten Ausgabe, Munich 1965

Sven Hedin, *Durch Asiens Wüsten, Drei Jahre auf neuen Wegen in Pamir, Lop-nor, Tibet und China, fünfte Auflage*, Leipzig 1915

Bruno Zoratto, *Inferno Tibet, Gespräch mit dem Friedensnobelpreisträger 1989*, Böblingen 1990

FRENCH BOOKS

Tibet, Des Journalistes Temoignent,La Maison du Tibet, Paris 1992

Register of People